IT'S NOT ABOUT THE MONEY

IT'S NOT ABOUT THE MONEY

BOB PROCTOR

 **BURMAN**BOOKS

Published by BurmanBooks Inc.
260 Queens Quay West
Suite 904
Toronto, Ontario
Canada M5J 2N3

Editing:
Murray Scott

Distribution:
Trumedia Group
c/o Ingram Publisher Services
14 Ingram Blvd.
LaVergne, TN 37086

ISBN 978-1-897404-02-7

Printed in Canada

This book is dedicated to

Gina Hayden

Gina has been a tireless worker with me for close to 25 years. She has supported me in every project I have been involved with all over the world. Our company would have never accomplished what we have without her. Everyone at LifeSuccess Productions and Bob Proctor Seminars loves her and appreciates her.

Thank you Gina.

Acknowledgments

I am a firm believer that anyone who has ever achieved anything of great consequence has not done it alone—they are backed by an incredible team.

I have been very fortunate in my life to have attracted a phenomenal cadre of mentors. My special thanks to my early mentors, Raymond Stanford, Val Van De Wall, Dr. Harry Roder and Bill Gove who taught me as much about myself as they did about business. And to my mentors, Earl Nightingale and Lloyd Conant, many thanks for the wonderful education I received about our industry in the five years I spent with the Nightingale-Conant Corporation.

To my business partners who handle the day to day operations of our various companies—special thanks to:

Paul Martinelli, Cheryl Fisher and staff who work with and train our LifeSuccess Consultants and licensees to effectively teach our materials worldwide.

Carol and Dan Gates, who with the assistance of Barb Duthie and Margaret Merrill, have developed our year-long coaching program which operates globally—teaching individuals to be more, do more and have more.

Gerry Robert, my son Raymond and their dedicated team who run our Publishing division, showing entrepreneurs the benefits of using a book as a marketing tool.

Sandy Gallagher-Alford and staff, who head up our Corporate division in helping small businesses and corporations alike develop their most precious resource—their people.

Tiffany Baron, Amzi Marsh, and staff for your work in The Chairman's Club—a company whose focus is assisting people in creating more wealth in their lives by setting up Multiple Sources of Income and joint ventures worldwide.

The staff in LifeSuccess Perfect Weight—a division of our company dedicated to health and wellness.

Kim Klein, Darron Yancy and their phenomenal team in accounting for keeping everything in order; God knows it's not easy with me at the helm! Deb White and the sales team for the incredible job they do in making people aware of our products and services. Jim Pallister and staff for keeping up with the ever changing world of the internet!

Mark Low—you're one of the best salespeople I've ever come across.

Renate van Dijken and Joost Oolders in LifeSuccess Youth, who have built a safe online environment that makes our materials available for FREE to young people worldwide.

My son Brian who came to me several years back with an idea of sending out a motivational quote each day and who has built Insight of the Day which offers motivation, inspiration and education via an array of quotes, stories and personal development programs marketed through the internet.

Mark Meyerdirk, Gina Hayden and Pixie Low who handle the day to day running of our holding company, LifeSuccess Productions and who make sure I'm where I should be.

Thank you to Rhonda Byrne of The Secret for inviting me to participate in an exceptional project and for the role you have played in the personal development industry.

Thank you to my good friends for allowing me to mastermind and learn from you—John Assaraf, Michael and Rickie Beckwith, Jack Canfield, Mark Victor Hansen, Shirley Hunt, Vic Johnson, Cynthia Kersey, Mary Morrissey, Murray Smith, Jane Willhite, and Doug Wead.

To my publisher, Sanjay Burman, and all who assisted in the production of this book—Dee Burks, Jack Steiner, John Manikaros and Murray Scott—my sincere thanks to you.

And finally, to my wife, Linda, whose happy disposition and loving heart has enriched my life in more ways than I could have ever imagined.

Table of Contents

Foreword

Internalize the ideas in this book and apply them wisely; if you do so, you can get everything you want in your life. These ideas are that powerful. You have a virtual gold mine right here on these pages. The key is wise application.

As I sat down to write this, it suddenly dawned on me what I was about to do. I was going to introduce you to some of the most transformational information that you will find anywhere. Then it also flashed on my mind that you have attracted this. You were supposed to have this book in your hands. But it wasn't the book that you attracted. It was the information that lies between its covers. Everything comes into your life by law. So don't just open this book and go quickly from page to page and then lay the book down. Rather, make a decision right now that you are going to study every page. You might spend an hour on a page and you might do that frequently; I do. Take the information that you are studying and relate it to how you are presently living and what you are doing, that way you will see where changes in your behavior will improve your entire life.

Internalize the jewels of wisdom that lie here in these lines waiting for you. Act on them and enjoy the benefits that the author promises you will receive as you go from one magnificent idea to the next. When you lay this book down having gone through it thoroughly, you are going to be walking away a freer, more dynamic individual, expressing the power that is and always has been at the center of your being. You see, your belief system will change. You'll have a deeper, more meaningful understanding of who you are, how your mind functions, and how to continue moving to a higher and higher level of conscious awareness.

Now before I go any further introducing you to the information in this book, I want to go back and let you think of where this information came from. The author's own life made a dramatic shift when he was 26 years old. The change in his results was so remarkable that he couldn't be satisfied with the tremendous rewards he was receiving. He wanted to know why. Why him? What happened? How did it happen? And this set him on a journey that he is still on today. In the process there has been 48 years of intense research that has gone into why we do what we do and why we don't do many of the things we really want to do. Bob Proctor's mentors have been some of the wisest people that have lived in the past 500 years. He has studied their lives like a scientist, meticulously analyzing their great ideas and doing exactly what they suggested.

I suppose if there was a way that we could determine just how many years of intense study went into the development of the information you are holding in your hands, the formula would have to take into consideration all of the authors Bob Proctor has studied and the authors they in turn studied. If we squared Bob Proctor's 48 years of intense study, we might come close, yet even then we would probably fall short. That is not nearly as important as it is for you to understand that all of this information that you are about to uncover has been tested and re-tested; it has stood the test of time. It has helped the author earn millions, and he in turn has helped others earn many more millions. You have a virtual gold mine right here on these pages, but you must apply it. And, to truly capitalize on it, you will have to share it with everyone who is open enough to receive it.

You see, I know what I am telling you is factual because after decades of intellectual development while obtaining my law degree, practicing corporate law and putting acquisitions and other transactions together for my clients, I discovered these ideas and then the various pieces of the puzzle to my life suddenly fit together. My discovery occurred in August 2006 when I was fortunate to attend one of Bob Proctor's seminars in Vancouver, Washington. That event changed the course of my life. I knew from that day forward I would spend the rest of my days finding ways to share the powerful ideas that Bob teaches.

It wasn't until discovering these ideas that I was able to understand why I had achieved the many successes in my life. Studying this material helped me understand that *everything that happens on the outside is first originated on the inside.* From a young age, I had been following what Bob Proctor was teaching. I was living in harmony with the laws of the universe with respect to my own personal goals, but if someone asked me why I was doing well, I couldn't answer them. Now I am able to show others how to enjoy life to the degree that I am enjoying life now, and have for many years, and I love that idea. What I wish for you is that these ideas that Bob Proctor shares in this book will do for you what they have done for me.

I want to leave you with advice that Emerson gave us, a line that I found to be literally accurate, and as you internalize this book you will as well. He said:

"What lies before you and what lies behind you are tiny matters compared to what lies within you."

Sandy Gallagher, B.A., J.D.
CEO, LifeSuccess Group of Companies
Bellevue, Washington

Introduction

It's Not About The Money can show anyone, who has a desire to learn, how to transform virtually every aspect of his or her life.

Bob Proctor's best-selling book *You Were Born Rich* has inspired individuals worldwide to live and afford the life they truly desire. Now, with *It's Not About The Money*, a fresh approach during a critical economic change is available to readers who are attempting to bring new order and balance to their life.

I believe one reason for the popularity of Bob's approach is that he speaks to the true potential that lies within all of us. He touches the reader in a deep, personal manner as well as a universal one. I would like to draw on my personal experience in this introduction, in order to show how anyone can add a new dimension of meaning and prosperity to their life by following his teachings.

You are about to embark on an experience that will forever change the way you think about money. The secret to wealth creation will be revealed to you in *It's Not About The Money*.

The Man Behind The Book

What you are about to read is the synthesis of Bob Proctor's more than 40 years of experience as a teacher, mentor and speaker on the subject of money and the mind. He has studied under some of the greatest pioneers of self –development, and now we have the privilege of learning from the knowledge he has accumulated and applied over decades.

It is important to consider Proctor's background. He was raised in poverty, lacked formal education, was rejected job after job and had no substantial business experience. All odds of success were against him. Yet, when you take a look at what he has accomplished over the last 40 years it will cause you to wonder. Most people would say it is astounding; although, I can attest from personal experience that Bob Proctor does not think of his accomplishments as being astounding. He is genuinely of the opinion that what he has done anyone can do. As a result of his background and life experience, Bob Proctor has been able to shatter the myths about money that have kept the majority of the world's population in bondage.

I, in turn, had followed a very orthodox path. I graduated from high school, earned a Bachelor's Degree in college, then went on to become an Electrical Engineer taking a position in a large corporation. Yet despite working as a professional for a number of years, I was unhappy, bored and barely able to pay the bills. At that time I bought into the idea that if I just worked harder, put in more hours and got another job I would earn a lot of money. Instead, I ended up burnt-out, miserable and with no time left in my day to enjoy anything outside of work.

It was at this point in my life that I was introduced to Bob Proctor. As I started to study his material, I began to realize I had some erroneous beliefs about money, especially the earning of money. My life began to seriously change when I realized that regardless of a person's background or experience, earning a substantial amount of money begins with building an image in the mind. Like the chair you are sitting in or the room you are standing in, both originated as an idea, or thought, in someone's mind.

Today, I have a totally different outlook on money. I went from working in a tiny cubicle to now running a global company with Bob Proctor called the Chairman's Club, a company designed to show people all over the world how to accumulate great fortunes by setting up Multiple Sources Of Income.

Bob Proctor's teachings have literally caused my entire life to change dramatically, and as you begin to read *It's Not About The Money*, your life too will begin to change.

What Is Money?

As you read this book, know that your awareness will begin to shift, and you will arrive at the truth that money is an idea. Money makes a great servant but a terrible master. Money provides two sole purposes, which are to make you comfortable and to enable you to provide service far beyond your physical presence.

Your ability to earn money will grow as your awareness grows. Bob Proctor often asks people what the most amount of money is that they have ever earned in a year. He does that, not to know how much money they have earned, but rather, to see where their level of awareness is with respect to earning money. If you were aware of how to earn in a month what it currently takes you a year to acquire with little or no more effort, would you do it? Yes of course!

Relish The Book

The best use of this book is to make it a study. I remember seeing Bob Proctor pulling out a book while on stage at one of his seminars. The cover kept falling off, the pages were aged in color and condition, sections were highlighted or underlined and hand-written notes were visible throughout the book. Bob then made the statement that he had been continuously reading the book he held in his hand for over 40 years. I believe *It's Not About The Money* is a book that we should read over and over again, year after year. Let yourself get emotionally involved with the ideas you read. Think of ways you can put into action all that you learn. Lastly, sit down, relax and be prepared to give up every preconceived notion you have about money. Let yourself be guided by the wisdom and principles shared in this book, for it will lead you to all that you truly desire.

Tiffany Baron, B.S.E.Engr.
President, Chairman's Club
Phoenix, Arizona

Chapter 1

Money Is Not the Goal

There's a book that's very important to me, one I've been reading, over and over, since I first got it in 1961. It's Napoleon Hill's *Think and Grow Rich*, one of the real groundbreakers in my field. It's inspiring, absolutely, and Hill is a great thinker who had a profound effect on my life. But the most important thing about that book? Hill delves into all kinds of topics, stories, examples and exercises—*but he doesn't really talk about money.*

This might seem strange for a book about "growing rich." But here's another one: *You Too Can Be Prosperous*, by Robert Russell. Another great author, and again, it hasn't got much to do with money at all. I hope you're getting the picture here: One of the keys to creating wealth for yourself is to understand that money is not the goal. Let me repeat that, for emphasis: **Money is not the goal**.

What these authors have come to understand is that creating wealth has very little to do with focusing on money. Really, what it has to do with is your mind, your attitude, and the way you think.

It sounds so simple, but most people really just don't grasp it, even though it's as plain as the nose on your face. Think about it: When you think of living a wealthy life, what comes to mind? Is it a home on a tropical island? Your own airplane? Doing whatever you want, whenever you want? All of these, maybe—and more?

That's my guess. And I bet I'm right. But did you imagine piles of cash, or 7, 8, 9-digit bank accounts? I would think not. Think of it this way: Webster's Dictionary defines wealth as "an abundant supply." It doesn't say an abundant supply *of money*, does it?

Money only has value because we believe it to. It's printed on paper that is actually quite worthless. So when someone says to me that they want to make a lot of money, what I hear is that they want the things money can be traded for: the cars, the islands, the planes. But most of all, they're pursuing the ultimate luxury: the freedom of time to enjoy it.

So when I say that money is not the real goal, this is precisely what I mean. The goal is not simply amassing wealth, but rather, an ongoing journey of growth, both personal and financial. This can be a tough concept for many of us to grasp. After all, we've been taught our whole lives that the point of making money is to accumulate as much as we can.

But that's looking at it backwards. I'm sure you've heard the phrase "money can't buy you happiness." Well, that is just about the most absurd statement I've ever heard. That's like saying you can't ride around town on a refrigerator. The statement is equally as ridiculous. Of course money can't buy you happiness—but what it can do is make you comfortable enough that you no longer need to think about it.

Money consumes us if we don't have it. The price of most products and services is continually increasing and I could care less. Why should I worry about something over which I have absolutely no control? But if I didn't have money, I'd sure be thinking about it.

It consumes our time and our energy. It reduces our infinite mental and creative powers to a worry machine. This is why you need to break out of this cycle and stop making excuses. This is why you need to realize money is not the goal.

When I think about people who have made great successes for themselves, I don't see people who chase money. I see people who understand the mind. They aren't thinking about earning money. They're focused on what they're doing.

This is where you have to understand that the path to wealth is a mental game you need to play with yourself. "Money can't buy you happiness?" That's a defensive statement we learn to make to justify to ourselves why we don't have it! In a moment of truth, you know you want to change that. This book will help show you how.

Wealthy people already understand that it's not about the money. They know it's not a goal unto itself. That's why you see them using money as a commodity of exchange rather than hording it.

So many of us have a hard time understanding this. But it's easy to see why. Our whole lives, we've been programmed to think money is the end goal. It's also why, when it doesn't come easily, we become defensive and make excuses for ourselves.

One of the easiest ways to show how money really works is to think of it as though it were water. A drop by itself is nothing. It's tiny, powerless. Think of it as a single dollar, if you would like. Not much can be done with it.

However, as the drops gather, they gain mass and momentum. They flow into small streams and then into rivers creating a torrent of abundance. This abundance has moved mountains and carved vast canyons. It has literally shaped our entire planet—but only as long as it's in motion. If it stops and pools, if there's no inward and outward flow, it stagnates and abundance begins to evaporate. The same is true of money.

Many people think you need to have a great deal of money to accomplish anything of value. This simply isn't true. Just like water, even small amounts of money applied in the right way can be deceptively powerful. Only a small amount of water rushing in a mountain stream can knock you off your feet! The secret is not in the amount, but the motion.

Money works in exactly this same way. As small amounts are invested in opportunities that produce cash flow, they come together to form a river, which provides a constant stream of wealth. Those who know this *Law of Circulation* understand that they are a conduit for money to flow through, not a stopping point.

The Difference Between Them and You

When the average person looks at the very wealthy—millionaires, or even billionaires—he or she assumes there's something unique or special about them, that they're more intelligent and savvy than 'normal people.' This assumption is both true and false.

They're wealthy because they have thoroughly internalized the mindset of wealth, and that can never be taken from them. If they lost everything and went broke, they would get back on their feet and become wealthy again, because they've come to understand how money works. That understanding is imprinted on the sub-conscious mind—much like the wrong information is imprinted on the sub-conscious of most everyone else. This is an idea we'll be getting to soon.

But other than that very fundamental difference, the wealthy are like everyone else. They live and work, laugh and love and have ups and downs just like you do. They have the exact same number of hours in the day as everyone else; but they do quite astonishing things with their time while most of us do very little.

So what's the difference? Not very much. And yet, it's *everything*—how you think, feel and what you believe about money.

We all know the cliché 'seeing is believing.' I'm telling you right now that that is a very skeptical and negative view of the abundant and limitless opportunities life has to offer you. It tells you you can only trust what's in front of your nose, and pays short shrift to the significant—even limitless—powers of your imagination, your intuition and creative self.

And yet, we hear it our whole lives over and over. It becomes a part of our thought process and we don't even know it. Wealthy people understand that this cliché is exactly backward—before you see what you want, you have to internalize it. You must believe in what you can achieve—only then will you see it happen. In other words, wealthy people follow the credo that 'believing is seeing.' The only thing that makes you different from a billionaire right now is a wealthy mindset. And the cornerstone of that mindset is *belief*.

It's said that wealthy people attract wealth. We know this to be true. How do they do it? They expect it. In their mind, no doubts cloud their goal, nothing causes them to pause or hesitate. They don't worry about failure because, in their mind's eye, all they can see is success.

Earlier on, I mentioned *Think and Grow Rich* by Napoleon Hill. I still carry a copy with me everywhere, and I read at least a small bit each day. Hill interviewed hundreds of successful, wealthy people and discovered that while each of them had become successful in a different way, they all had a certain mindset in common. Because they expected success, they attracted opportunities that others did not. They were able to see solutions that others could not.

Does this mean that the wealthy were born with some special skill or a sixth sense? Not at all. It simply means that they are more aware. Gaining this awareness, as a friend of mine once said, is simple—it's just not easy. There's a fundamental reason why.

It has to do with your mind. Most of us grow up in fundamentally the same way: we go to school, we learn a skill, we get a job and we live our lives. That accounts for 90 percent of the population. I would suggest that that same percentage has no idea how to earn money.

Ask a person on the street if they know how to earn money, and you'll get the same answer 99 times out of 100. "Of course I know how to earn money. I go to work every day." But that's not earning money. That's getting a job and grinding out a living. There's a big difference.

There's such a small percentage of our population that knows how to *earn money*. There's a reason for that. School doesn't teach it. We learn how to count money. We make balance sheets, graphs and charts. We account for every last penny. You can have a doctorate degree in economics and still be broke because you never learn how to *earn money*.

School prepares us to get a job. It programs our mind that this is how the world works. It tells us this is the safe path. It tells us this is how we'll be secure. Your parents told you that. Your schoolteachers told you that. I had a teacher who told me to go to tech school and earn a trade. That way, she said, I'd be secure.

I didn't listen. For one thing, I hate trade work. For another, I'm no good at it. I almost cut my finger off with a band saw once and it still hurts! And finally, the truth is, working is one of the worst ways to earn money and one of the least secure.

Work hard. Be loyal. You'll be rewarded. That's what we were told from the very beginning. Well, the reward for too many of us is to show up one day to find that the locks have been changed and all you've got is a small severance after 18 years of loyal service. There isn't any security in a job. Security comes from within. And that's where you need to find it. If you believe there's security in a job and you lose your job, you're going to be totally demoralized because you've lost everything.

It comes back to being aware of who we are and changing the programming. Most people get stuck in what they're doing. It's almost like we don't want to admit that we don't know how to earn money. It's easy enough to sweep under the carpet. After all, we're getting paid, aren't we?

And that's why these ridiculous stories arise: 'Money can't buy happiness.' That's what we tell ourselves when we don't want to take responsibility for not earning as much as we would like.

What we need to do is abandon the excuses and open our mind. This comes from being aware of ourselves. Your results are an expression of your level of awareness. Imagine how your life would change if your awareness expanded: People don't earn $50,000 a year because they want to earn $50,000 a year. They earn $50,000 a year because they're not aware of how to earn $50,000 *a month*.

But, we can expand our level of awareness. The more we do that, the more we're going to win. The wealthy already have this awareness. It's hard-wired in them. In order to gain this same awareness, you need to understand why the wealthy have it and why it is so key to their success.

The first of these characteristics is a willingness to listen to their own inner wisdom. If listening to the masses made you rich, then the masses would be rich! But, we all know this is not the case.

As human beings who are sensitive and spiritual in nature, it is the most natural impulse in the world to seek counsel from those close to us—our loved ones, our close friends and colleagues.

We also need to look at the results they've had in their own lives before we follow their advice. We follow their advice because of the emotional trust we have in them, rather than on what they've achieved. If someone hasn't become wealthy, can they really show you how to become wealthy? Of course not.

You need to believe what is already the truth. Within you is the ability to create a unique path to fabulous wealth. You have to trust yourself and seek out only those who have traveled such a path to help guide your journey.

You also have to be willing to let the comments of critics and naysayers slide off your back. There will be many who will tell you your dreams are unrealistic and your goals too far-fetched.

And 'seeing is believing' leads you directly to a life only based on perception—and for many of us it can be a life we hate. Make a promise now. Listen to yourself first. Reality is what you make it.

The wealthy have the consistent ability to act when opportunities present themselves. Most people think of opportunity as something that arrives with great fanfare—a blaring, obvious event that assaults you with its obviousness. It's almost as though we expect a giant neon sign flashing the word "opportunity" to appear with a brilliantly-lit arrow to point the way.

It doesn't work that way. That's where awareness becomes important. I know from personal experience that opportunity slips past each of us every day. Sometimes it's a whisper that comes during some of the most trying times of your life.

Successful people often view defeats and failures as opportunities...not obstacles. Their resumes are often messy— they've been fired, thrown out of school. They've often faced significant personal tragedies that would sink the average person— maybe for good. But these people chose to see these trials as challenges to be met and opportunities to be grasped. As a result, through adversity, they prosper.

The wealthy also understand that wealth is a process. It rarely happens overnight (though it certainly has). However, there's a danger in sudden wealth. If you become rich before you've developed the wealthy mindset, then you stand in danger of losing that wealth forever.

We've all heard about lottery winners who end up penniless a few years later. Our culture is filled with celebrities and athletes whose sudden rush to fame and fortune leads them to squanderous lifestyles that leaves them poor with much of their lives left to live.

These people were never taught to think wealthy. Because of that, they have almost no chance of achieving lasting wealth that frees your mind from the preoccupations and distractions of money forever.

Remember, at the beginning, when I said **money is not the goal**? Hold on to that thought. It will always be your guide. If you have a wealthy mindset, you do what you love—and make money doing it. It's not the goal—it's the result.

I often meet people who are searching for a way to be wealthy, as though it was something out in the world that you could hunt down, trap and keep. In truth, wealth exists inside you. There are things you love to do Those are the things you would happily do even if you were being paid nothing to do them. Well, guess what? The people that create a great deal of wealth are doing exactly that. The money that follows is the logical result of them following their dream. Money is not the dream. We're all hard wired to do something. And we need to find a way to do that "something".

Wealthy people know that success and responsibility go hand in hand. They don't make excuses; they take action. How often have you seen two people in the exact same business, in the exact same location, selling the exact same product—but one is wealthy and the other struggles?

The circumstances are the same. What a certain person makes of those circumstances in entirely up to them. There is no such thing as lack of potential. We're taught exactly the opposite—that some people don't have a good memory or that some are smarter than others. Nonsense! Everyone has a perfect memory and the wealthy are not superhuman geniuses. Everyone can achieve wealth—it's a matter of developing the skill. I cannot stress this enough: **There is no such thing as lack of potential.**

It doesn't matter how many times I explain it or how many times you read it or listen to it on my CDs. Your life will never change until you truly and honestly believe it. Believing is seeing. That is the basic truth and you need to embrace it before you can go any further.

Without it, changing your mindset simply can't happen. You may have a mindset right now that is a barrier to achieving the wealth you want. Think about it for just a second. If you're honest with yourself the simplest questions will reveal your programming to you.

Now, let me ask you—are you comfortable talking about money with others? Or, does it make you edgy, as though it's something to talk about in whispers as though it was taboo? When you talk about money, do you shrug off questions about how much you earn and what you can afford as though they were unimportant? Do these subjects make you feel awkward and out of place?

You wouldn't be the only one. Most of us feel that way when we talk about money because so few of us are where we want to be with our personal wealth and pursuit of it. But remember... believing is seeing. Think about how wealthy people talk about money. They're completely comfortable with it. It is no different than any other subject of interest in their lives that they embrace and chat about with gusto.

They allow their ideas about money to flow freely and exchange them with like-minded people. This exchange often results in ways to create new and diverse income sources, which in turn increases their wealth. They're not embarrassed to talk about money. They don't attach emotion to it. They are comfortable with something that makes most of us uneasy.

There's a really simple reason for this. Remember what we said at the beginning? **Money is not the goal.** It's a tool to achieve our real goal of living our lives according to our dreams and starting to grasp our limitless potential. Financial success is not wealth. It's a consequence of achieving real wealth. That's what separates the truly wealthy from the rest of us: finances, employment status and time constrains do not control their path to success. Believing is seeing—and they are absolutely focused on these ultimate goals.

Many of us get in our heads that being wealthy will require sacrifices we don't want to make such as working harder and being away from our families. But sacrificing all our freedom and neglecting those most important to us is the opposite of leading a wealthy life, isn't it? Remember, wealth isn't just about generating money. It's doing what you love in the way you want to do it. The goal of a wealthy life is to create the freedom that puts the power in your hands—the power to choose the life you want.

The Prison of Perception

But how? I hear this question constantly. How can I think wealthy when I'm dirt poor? How can I imagine a wealthy life when I'm stuck in a dead-end job I hate? How can I invest my money in opportunities when every dime I have is needed to keep my family going?

These kinds of thoughts poison the wealthy mindset. They infect your ability to believe, and see, where you need to go and what you need to do.

These questions make plain for everyone that the person asking them has a long way to go before their own wealthy mindset can be achieved. They're locked in a prison they've made for themselves, and they've thrown away the key. They've convinced themselves they can't achieve their own dreams. Why on earth would anyone do such a horrible thing to themselves?

And yet, so many of us do just that, day in and day out. That prison is a crowded place. I call it the Prison of Perception. Those prison walls aren't real at all—they only appear to stand in the way.

We build the walls of our own private cell with bricks made up of assumptions and ideas accumulated over a lifetime. I'm sure you're familiar with many of them:

- I'm not smart enough
- I don't have enough money
- I don't have enough time
- I didn't graduate college
- I'm afraid to fail
- I'm too old
- I'm too young

These negative thoughts make their way into the mind by repetition until your sub-conscious—that wonderful, spiritual place where emotion resides and where anything is possible—is so weighed down with them that they dictate what you actually think. As negative things happen throughout your life, they're reinforced and their power grows. This is why most of us are convinced we can never live a wealthy life. In our sub-conscious mind, we're programmed to believe it.

Many of us are captives of our own prisons and it is entirely in our mind. Over time, as we build our own captivity, we convince ourselves that this tiny space is all we can have and all we deserve.

Changing this mindset is difficult. It takes time. Serious work is required to overtake these assumptions. After all, they're both genetic and environmental. It goes back many generations. That's why we look like our relatives. And, in our little life, from the moment we were born, we were being conditioned environmentally.

As I said before, the societal norm is to go to school, get a job, and do what we can to get by. Your parents probably encouraged you to do that. Your schoolteachers certainly did. If this is your programming, how can you be to blame for the prison that results?

I came upon these concepts almost by chance. Remember when I said I had a teacher who tried to talk me out of education and to learn a trade instead? Well, I didn't do either. I never finished high school. It was 1959. I was pumping gas and making

$2400 a year. I had three Sundays off a month—that was it. I knew I wanted more, but I hadn't figured out how to get it. So I did what most people do: I looked for another job.

I managed to talk myself onto the fire department in my local community and things immediately looked up. I was making $4000 a year and I thought I'd died and gone to heaven. I only worked seven days and seven nights a month. I had all the time in the world to shoot pool and play golf. Fires were very rare so I was content to do almost nothing.

Here I was 26 years old and virtually retired. Then, I got my hands on Napoleon Hill's book. I read it once. Then I read it again. I kept reading it and reading it, over and over, until I could practically repeat it verbatim. And slowly, I started to realize that, like myself, the people around me were doing nothing— they weren't thinking. They weren't thinking about where they wanted to be or what they wanted to do. They were content to do what they were told when they had to, and do nothing the rest of the time.

It was like a light bulb switched on in a dark room. My income went from $4000 a year to $175,000, and then over a million. I never went to school and I had no business experience. I wouldn't describe myself as the smartest guy in the world, either—that's why I study other people.

Absolutely everything I had been taught about success and achieving wealth told me I couldn't possibly win. And yet, I was winning. That's when I realized that most of the things we're taught are simply not correct. Rather than think what we want to think and believe what we want to believe, we let outside influences control what's going on in the inside world—the world of our mind. That causes confusion and produces results that we really don't want.

If most of us took the time to think for a moment, we'd realize that the concepts controlling our lives are ridiculous! But we don't, so we just keep going and are blind to the walls of the prison cell we've built around ourselves.

This is what we need to change. It's not easy. In fact, you'll struggle with it your entire life. This is why you have to practice and internalize that believing is seeing. Commit to it. Truly accept it and it will get easier and easier as you move towards your dreams.

There are things you can do immediately to get started. These are the first steps in what will become a way of life—a wealthy life. I'm telling you these things, here and now, so you can get started right this very minute to change your life. I'll explain them in greater detail as we move on, but there's no reason you can't start to apply these things and get started on your journey *right now*. No more wasted time doing nothing.

Ready?

First, you need to believe that you *deserve* wealth. This seems so simple, and yet, so many people can't grasp it. We give money too much credit The fact is, money is simply a reward for a service rendered. If you're going to earn a lot of it, you need to provide a lot of service. You can do this. It's your right to exercise if you choose to, just like anybody else—like those millionaires and billionaires you read about. It's not enough to say you want wealth—you have to believe you deserve it, too. Otherwise, it's like driving with one foot on the brake and another on the gas—the engine races but you don't go anywhere.

For a lot of people, the pursuit of wealth gets tangled up in all sorts of negative emotions—it's greedy and self-serving or it can destroy a person's sense of self. But like the notion that money can't buy you happiness, these kinds of negative emotions around wealth are simply excuses to make you feel better about not having it.

Here's the truth: having more money won't change you as a person. It will, however, magnify *the person you already are*. Money has a remarkable ability to reveal character. If you're stingy and cruel, money will expose those negative traits completely so they are unmistakeable and obvious. But if you're a generous spirit, someone who is caring and giving and compassionate to those around you, think of what wealth will allow you to achieve!

Money will never give you certain traits. This is important to remember when you come across wealthy people who are mean or unkind. It's easy for us to blame the wealth for the person's shortcomings, when in fact it's their intractable character—rich or poor—that has simply risen to the surface.

You'll remember I spoke about the wealthy mindset. Part and parcel in that, in my mind, is to enter into your pursuit of wealth with a generosity of spirit and all the creative curiosity you have. Why? Because the only way to earn money is to provide something—a product, a service, even an idea—that brings unrealized value to other people's lives. Think about how you can tackle the challenges of everyday life and then make them faster, more efficient or even more fun for people. The bigger the problem you solve, the more money will stream in.

Historically, wealthy people have always had multiple sources of income (MSIs). In other words, they have found multiple ways of providing service. I started a company, some time ago, to assist people in this area. The company is called The Chairman's Club and it's attracted like-minded people from all over the world who work together to set up multiple sources of income. The Chairman's Club has an online global communications center where the various members meet and share new ways to create income. This might be something you would like to investigate. For information go to www.BobProctorMoney.com/CC.

In my mind, you don't share ideas with other people when you're self-interested and closed-minded. You do that, as I've said, by pursuing what you love. Think about Bill Gates. Here was a young man in the late 70s who was really driven by the massive unrealized potential of the microcomputer chip. I would argue

Bill Gates was not driven by money, but the incredible challenge he set for himself, and the amazing possibility that, if he achieved it, he could change the world!

Well, that's exactly what he did. Some may say he doesn't deserve all the wealth he now enjoys. But the fact is, Bill Gates started a revolution that improved the quality of life for virtually everyone in the world. Regardless of how much money he may possess, it will never equal his true contribution to humanity, which was forever changed by his spirit of innovation.

He's an icon now. But 30 years ago, he was a college dropout with a clever idea. He looked around his world and identified a way to make people's lives better. Then he acted on that dream and made it reality. You can start where you are right now and develop more valuable skills, network with wealthy mentors and focus on serving people. From these actions will come the ideas that will be your specific and unique path to wealth.

As you create a new awareness of wealth and come across new opportunities, start thinking of those opportunities with passive income in mind. It's a key concept: Passive income is something you do once and get paid for multiple times. Think about it. If all you do is exchange your time for money, your wealth is limited. After all, there are only so many hours in a day.

How do you solve this problem? You create sources of income that don't demand your constant presence and attention. While those sources of income flow to you, you can use your valuable time hunting out ways to create more.

I've already mentioned that belief is the cornerstone of a wealthy mindset. So how do you create this belief of wealth even if it seems very far-fetched right now? First, you have to *visualize yourself with wealth*. Really sit and actively think about the details of your life that wealth will alter when you reach your goals. Write them down: the type of house you'll live in, the color of the walls and the style of the furniture, the china you'll eat off of and the silverware you'll use to serve it. In your mind, make them real, not abstract. Clip pictures from magazines and use them to build your new home in your new life. Every day spend some time there using those images to transport you to it, as though you already owned it.

Some might call this daydreaming. I'm willing to bet those people aren't wealthy! The truth is, visualizing lets your mind grab hold of the possible. It trains your mind to the idea that your life is changing and that wealth is within reach. Once you harness the power of your mind, it's not just within reach—it's inevitable!

Some people are surprised to learn the wealthy spend much of their time just quietly thinking. Employees might watch their boss or CEO staring off into space. They might think he or she is doing nothing at all. In fact, that person is visualizing the next phase of their wealth and success, the next mountain to climb— and of course, they're watching themselves reach the top!

They know that innovation and creativity—the next big thing that will take them and their company to the next level— isn't found in mundane daily operations. That's why they have employees. The wealthy mindset has taught them that new ideas are the lifeblood of wealth and visualizing them come to fruition is essential. How can you get where you're going if you haven't clearly decided what your destination is? When a wealthy person reaches their goal, it is exactly what they expected—precisely because, through visualization, *they've already been there.*

Would you get in the car and start driving when you're not sure where you're going? Of course not. You'd look at a map, chart your path and start on your way. But many, many people live their lives without that map and just take whatever comes across their path in life. They work at jobs they hate and never imagine a better way. They accept the familiar simply because they have never taken the time to *see past it.*

You must remember that visualization is a very positive exercise. It brings your dreams from your unconscious mind into a place where your conscious mind can connect to them.

To do this effectively, you have to *banish negative thoughts from your mind*. This is easier said than done. Negative thinking is a bad habit practiced by far too many people. They like to complain about the state of their lives or careers or commiserate with friends and colleagues about all of their various dissatisfactions. They become convinced that this kind of negative thinking is good: If expectations are kept low, you can never be disappointed.

Well, I think this is the most ridiculous thing I've ever heard! How on earth did any of us reach the point where we convinced ourselves it was better not to dream? How on earth can you expect too much? Why would you scuttle your dreams and your goals before they even get off the ground?

Negative thinking has become the rule in our society. It is accepted and very widely practiced. So you have to make a serious and conscious effort to push these thoughts out of your mind. Be vigilant. Guard your mind from theses thoughts. They can only slow you down and get in your way. Be ruthless in what kind of thoughts you allow to take hold in your mind. If you focus on the positive—great ideas, spawned by your best, positive creative energies—you'll get great results.

But be careful. Monitor your internal dialogue closely— especially in terms of what other people tell you regarding money, finance and wealth. Remember to seriously consider dismissing their thoughts if they have not achieved wealth themselves. If you gain wisdom from someone truly wealthy, open your mind to it and make it part of your internal dialogue. Even if you don't understand it, or don't agree, keep it with you. After all, they've already traveled the road you've just started on. You wouldn't drive off to points unknown without a map; these people are that map. They know the path. Treat their words as bricks in the yellow brick road.

Be aware of your focus. If you say you want wealth but are constantly under attack from worry—about how to pay your bills, or make a mortgage payment, for example—you're not attracting wealth into your life. You're engaged in *a mindset of lack*. Worrying is negative goal-setting. By dwelling on the bad things that *could* happen, you're telling your mind what *will* happen!

It's visualization in reverse. By worrying about what you don't have, you're not focusing on what you want. If you do that, wealth will never be yours. Now, I know worry is a hard thing to combat. We all worry to a degree. So how do we achieve this shift in focus?

Put yourself in this position for a moment: You're a secretary with a boss who demands that no errors be made—ever. You may work under the threat that, if you make a single mistake, you'll be fired. Where's your focus—doing the best job you can, or trying your hardest not to make a mistake? If you're obsessed with the narrow task of not making a mistake, two things happen. First, the overall quality of your work suffers as the paranoia stifles your creativity and ability to think clearly, and secondly, you will find you are making more mistakes than you otherwise would because *your mind is focused on errors.*

Now take that same idea and think about how much time and energy you spend worrying about paying your bills. Do you constantly track and add up the expenses? Do you spend time shuffling or rearranging what to pay when?

Does it solve the problem of not having enough money? No, it doesn't. It zaps your creative energy and leaves no time or room to think about what will correct the problem or help you. It only brings more negative energy and frustration into your life. We'll discuss exactly how this works in a later chapter, but for right now it is important that you make every effort to shift your focus from what you don't have to what you want to have. I can't say this often enough: *Focus on the positive!*

Visualize your new life, remove negative thoughts and focus on the positive. By using just these three techniques, you'll start to see your life change right now—*today*. They will give you a foundation to build on and a quick jumpstart to your new life. Wealth doesn't discriminate. It is available to everyone who wants it—*including you*.

For many people, the revelation isn't in using these techniques—it is in understanding that they have the power and right to change their own lives for the better. We get so used to struggling through life, accepting whatever circumstances come our way, that we never realize that we have the power to choose our life.

There is no reason—and no excuse—to settle for a life that makes you unhappy. If you don't have enough money, or other elements of your life fall short of your desires, then you have to change your current mindset from one of lack to one of abundance. This means to shift from a victim mentality to one of responsibility and empowerment.

You *do* have control over your life. You have *chosen to be where you are now*. This is good news, believe me. You may not like where you are now, but now you know *you have the power to change it*!

What if you feel relatively happy with where you are now and just want to earn more money? Well, that's a great place to start. Wanting wealth does not mean that you are ungrateful or unhappy with your life. It's okay to want to reach higher, even if you've already come to a place where your life has many good things in it. As I've said, Our potential as humans is limitless, and in a perfect world, we are always trying to improve—to learn more, to know more, to achieve more.

The problem arises when others see you striving for more and read it incorrectly. They'll tell you striving comes from unhappiness. "Be content with what you have," they'll say. This is exactly the kind of backwards logic that unsuccessful people use to feel better about why they are not achieving more.

It implies that if you are not happy in your present circumstances, or desire more from life, that there is something wrong with you. This makes no sense. It is human to strive, seek and pursue. Making excuses to accept failure and encouraging other people to do the same is a self-defense technique that I urge you not to fall prey to. The desire to drag others down with us is the least humane behaviour of all.

The danger in this type of logic is that it convinces people to deny their desires and accept their lives as they are and not pursue those desires and dreams. These wrong-headed excuses let everybody off the hook. They absolve us of responsibility by stating it's okay to be a failure. Stay down here with me—It's easier.

But it's not. Denying your dreams and desires is the hardest path anyone could walk. Yet so many of us do it. I'm telling you to be bold. Accepting responsibility for creating a new future also means that you must accept that you have created your present life. This is very difficult for many people. I warned you up front that bringing about the shift to a wealthy mindset would not be easy. I told you that you would have to accept that you have control over your life and that your choices to this point have created the life you've lived so far. If you had any thoughts while reading this paragraph that begins with "Yes, but," then go back to the beginning of the chapter and read these pages again because you aren't getting it!

I don't say this to be harsh or mean. It's important to hear the truth. You have to listen, understand and ultimately accept this as truth in order to achieve what you want to achieve in this life. I'll never tell you it's okay to blame someone else. I can't tell you it's not your fault. I will never say you get a free pass because of things in your life that happened in the past. Please understand: there is no "Yes, but ... " to get what you want!

You have the power within to create vast wealth. If you haven't used it up until now, then you have no-one to blame but yourself. You have built your own *Prison of Perception*. But you—and you alone—have the power to break free.

Money Is Good

How often have you heard this: Money is evil. Wanting money is morally wrong. This is one lie that has prevented more good than could ever be imagined. Money has no emotion and no intent. It is only a medium of exchange. Any evil or moral aspect of money exists solely in the heart of each individual. That would be there with or without money. As I said before, money just pulls back the veil and reveals us all to be who we really are.

But many people harbor so much negativity concerning money that they sub-consciously reject it when opportunities come along. Even before they start on their way to a wealthy and abundant life, they have decided it's too hard or morally wrong. They do nothing and become spectators as others achieve their dreams.

Money can and should be associated with so many positive outcomes. By focusing on the positive you can rest assured that you will be in a position to reach your dreams—not just watch others reach theirs. One of these positive outcomes includes the ability to help others. This can include your family, friends, society or those in need. There are foundations and organizations that can improve the lives of people all over the world. By creating wealth, you aren't just helping yourself—you're creating a means to help these people, not to mention the people closest to you.

Wealth can give you the freedom of time to enjoy your life now. Too many of us spend our lives waiting—waiting for a two week vacation to spend time with family, waiting for those moments when you can do what you really want to do. That time is so short. It seems to fly by and in a flash it's gone. So we keep waiting. Another month, another year and the next thing you know the years have vanished before your eyes. If you are able to create wealth then you can spend time with your family or travel at any time you choose—not wait all year for those two short weeks of freedom. It's not really even freedom—it's just a short break from your year-long prison.

Creating ongoing sources of income gives you a great deal of self confidence. It bestows upon you a positive outlook for your future. It doesn't matter if family or government aren't able to help you in old age. You don't have to worry about that because your wealth means you'll always be taken care of.

Wealth allows you to be more generous and honest with others. I am sharing my knowledge of wealth with you in this book and I'm completely honest about every last point. Why? Because I've used these concepts and achieved these goals, and I know that others can benefit from what I've learned. As you create your own wealth, you'll do the same for others—share the path to wealth!

The human mind is the most powerful wealth creation tool that exists. It doesn't matter who you are. It doesn't matter what you've done up 'til now. It doesn't really even matter what you currently think you're capable of. Every time you think of money and wealth, think of all the positives associated with them. Through repetition these positive thoughts will be impressed upon your sub-conscious. You will feel very positive about money. You will attract opportunity like you never did before and wealth will follow easily and quickly into your life.

I mentioned the Chairman's Club; I started it specifically for that reason—to help people come up with ways to create new sources of income and mix with people who are doing the same (www.BobProctorMoney.com/CC).

Educate Yourself

Opportunities are of little use to us if we don't know how to take advantage of them. So we need to gain the knowledge of how to handle them or create them for ourselves.

This does not mean you need to go back to school. Most of my learning on wealth creation came from my own reading and my seeking knowledge with the focus I described earlier. There are a great many books, many of them wonderfully informative and clear-headed, written by some of the wealthiest people in the world. If you really want to, you can learn about opportunity by reading about those who have already seized theirs.

You can also seek out mentors who can give you sound advice and teach you the most effective strategies. But none of that matters if you don't have the right mindset. It's the most important part of success and it makes getting the knowledge you need that much easier. This is why I didn't mention education earlier. While it makes things a bit easier, it is not the most essential part of gaining wealth.

Just the other night, I was watching a show on TV that featured Donald Trump. He took questions and gave advice to a group of business school students. Now, Trump is very well-educated. But what's remarkable is that he made it very clear to these students that education is really secondary and the desire to succeed is much more important.

There may be people you know personally that are incredibly smart and hold numerous degrees but still aren't wealthy. Conversely, there may be some you know—and I myself know *many*—who have very little formal education and yet have experienced incredible success. So, if we put 2 and 2 together, we see that education does not determine wealth!

But if you have the right mindset and focus on increasing your wealth, then it is to your advantage to become more familiar with businesses that can create that wealth. Earning money is all about satisfying the wants and needs of others. Nothing is bought, sold or traded that does not satisfy a need or fulfill someone's desire. Finding ways to better serve your customers, business partners, colleagues, friends, family and others will lead you to the wealth you desire.

Keep this in mind and you'll see it reflected in your daily decisions and actions. Problems are encountered when you change your focus from cooperation with others to focusing strictly on yourself. When your thoughts concentrate on problems rather than solutions, you have slipped back into a negative thought pattern and your business will reflect it. Your problems are of no interest to the vast majority of people in your life; however, you can solve your own problems by simply helping others solve theirs.

People are self-involved by nature. But our problems are not as different as you might imagine. Even if you don't consider yourself a businessperson, satisfying the needs of others should be your primary objective in life. Most of your daily activities bring you in contact with all different types of people. If you focus on their needs, not yours, your success in life will grow exponentially in every area. And in the process, your own needs will be met automatically.

When I talk to anyone about changing their life, a common concern is risk. It's interesting that risk is seen as a concern. Wealthy individuals *do not consider themselves to be taking any risks at all*! In fact, what the average person might consider risk would not even be a passing concern to someone with a wealthy mindset. I like to talk about this subject last because risk is all about perception and fear.

Young children are not born with any sort of risk aversion— this behavior is entirely learned. If they were concerned with risk, they would never learn to walk, run or ride a bicycle. Think of the adventures you had as a child. How many involved risk? Almost every little boy (and most girls) that I know have at some point tied a sheet or towel around their neck, imagined they were a superhero and jumped—from the bed, from a tree, or even from the roof! The world of a child is full of adventure and open to infinite possibility. However, over time we are taught that risk is bad and the fear of what "might" happen overshadows the truth of what is.

How many people do you know who are afraid of flying in an airplane? There's always a few. If you ask them why, most will tell you they're afraid that the plane will crash. Now, it's a well-known fact that, statistically, you have a much higher chance of dying behind the wheel of your car than in an airplane crash.

Yet these same people don't think twice about driving. It is this *perception of risk* that limits their lives and causes much stress and anxiety—even though their fear is largely unfounded. I encounter the same wrong-headed rationale when I talk to people about becoming wealthy. Fear of the 'what ifs' clouds their judgment and shrinks their view of the possible.

One exercise I often use to help people move past this irrational fear is called "Then What?" If they say that they fear giving up their corporate job to start their own business, I ask them: "Well what would happen if you did?"

Either the business succeeds or it fails. Let's say it fails, then what? Then you close the door and find another job or another source of income. Then what? Are you any worse off than you are right now? No. Will your family starve to death and become homeless? No. What makes you think that the world will come to some sort of halt?

When we face uncertainty, it is easy to allow the fear to grow to irrational levels. The only way to combat this is to seriously think through the 'what ifs.' Quickly, you realize they are minor inconveniences at most. You *will* survive. You will *do at least as well* as you are right now. And there is every expectation that you will succeed and do even better!

When we struggle or experience difficult and challenging episodes, we need to be reminded that the tough times in our lives are temporary. There will always be a tomorrow. As long as you're still breathing, you will always have the chance to improve your life. Every day is a new opportunity to do exactly that. The perception that your life will be over, or come to some horrifying end, is only in your mind. It limits you, and serves to keep you locked within what you currently know.

The other idea I'd like to mention before we move on is this concept of "reality." The reality that you live today is the manifestation of all your past efforts. This is what has produced your present results. However, think of the disclaimer you see on stocks and mutual funds: "Past performance is not a guarantee of future results." Your future is open to infinite possibility; it is not dependent on the past. How you think today will determine the results you achieve from this point forward—*the past has no bearing on it*. Each decision you make and every thought you think are creating your future right now. Now is your chance to change that future for the better.

When others talk to you about reality, often they are speaking of the concept they have of you in their own mind—their own reality. They may also be projecting their fears onto you. But those perceptions—and those fears—have nothing to do with your ability to create the life of your dreams. Though their comments and cautions may be well-intended, they only slow you down. They convince you you are powerless. Listen to me: *You are not*. Whatever your own past, whatever you've done, whatever you've achieved and whatever opportunities you've missed along the way, *you can change your life starting right now*. The most important thing is your mindset and your desire to achieve the wealthy life of your dreams. The only 'reality' that matters is the one you create in your mind—right now, here, *today*.

For many years now I have operated Bob Proctor Coaching

(www.BobProctorMoney.com/BPC). It's a 13 month program where people are coached and educated on how to make the necessary changes within themselves to create the lifestyle they dream about. This reminds me of an interesting story from a serious student in our coaching program, Chris Guerriero. A couple of years after Chris completed the 13 month program, he wrote me a letter stating how dramatically his life had changed— and not just his, but the lives of everyone in his family. Chris explained how he had to put the investment on a couple of credit cards to pay for the coaching program and he said it was really worth it. I remember him saying, "I just had my first million dollar month." You see Chris always had that potential—what he had to do was properly utilize it.

Chapter 1 REVIEW

- Wealth is not about accumulation, it is about circulation.
- The only difference between you and a billionaire is a difference in mindset.
- Believing is Seeing—you must believe before you will see anything happen in your life.
- Money is not bad; it only enhances who you already are.
- Creating wealth is about adding value.
- Visualize your wealthy life on a continual basis.
- Remove negative thoughts from your mind and concentrate on the positive.
- Focus on what you want for your life rather than worrying about your problems.

Chapter 2

The Paradox

Top performers in all industries do what they do because they love to do it. For them, the work is its own reward. They understand how to create value and enjoy doing so. They don't work just to earn money. But it's also important to understand that they would not work for free. Looking from the outside in, this can be hard to understand. If the wealthy don't need any more money, and they're not working to gain more, then why do they do it?

A popular misconception has it that you accumulate money so you can stop working. But that's someone without a wealthy mindset talking. People ask me all the time when I might retire. My answer is, why would I stop doing what I love? To me, retirement means pulling back from life and giving up on something that enriches and fulfills my life every day. Why on earth would I do that?

While wealthy people talk a great deal about money and creating income, they almost never utter the word retirement. This is because the only people who long to retire are those who spend their lives in jobs they don't enjoy, or for which they have no passion.

By the same token, the idea that you should save for retirement strikes me as insane. The idea of saving for retirement is to deny yourself the life you want to live now so that you can hoard enough money to live the life you want in the future. That's backwards logic! The whole idea is surrounded with the fear of future lack of resources. The money and energy being hoarded could be put to much better use...creating ongoing sources of income that will continue for your entire life—no matter what your age or health.

The wealthy understand that work gives them energy and renews their passion for life. Take Warren Buffet. He made billions, and he has given billions away. Warren Buffet, you can be sure, doesn't need bigger, or more houses, cars or anything else. And you can bet he's not working so he can retire some day!

No, Warren Buffet works every day because he loves finding companies that provide products that customers need and that can bring value to his shareholders. That is his passion. And he is passionate about every phase of his business.

When you find a career or a business that you're truly passionate about, it no longer seems like work. It is an adrenaline rush. When you're great at what you do, what you do invigorates you every single day. That passion can help others to achieve their goals as well.

This is exactly how I feel about teaching people the principles that can change their lives for the better. I get up each morning enthused and anxious to get started. I anticipate great things will happen every single day—and they do! For me, there is no bigger thrill than helping someone understand the wealthy mindset, and then seeing them take that knowledge and become a millionaire.

Successful people are not unique. But the one thing they have in common is that they are passionate. They have developed the inner strength to maintain a consistent persistency. This allows them to go beyond the point where the average person would have given up. That's the wealthy mindset at work. It shows you how to see beyond the world of acceptable or average.

The Attitude of Average

What does it mean to be average? If you gathered one hundred random people in a room and asked them how they view themselves in relation to others, I would estimate that 97 of them would say that they are about average. The term average has taken on a meaning far beyond its actual definition. In fact, average represents the midpoint, and as such can only represent one number. This means, simply by definition, that out of your group of one hundred people, ninety-nine are not average. Think about that.

Does this mean that they're all lying? Not really. But 'average' has taken on a meaning that we often equate with 'normal' or 'acceptable.' Saying you're 'average' gives a sense of belonging to the masses—even if it is far from the truth. The problem is the idea becomes lodged in the mind. Then you see people who achieve great things to be very far above yourself. You believe they are special or lucky or know something that you don't. The difference between what you might consider an average life and a wealthy life is really quite small. Yet the *perception of difference is huge*!

It is this *Attitude of Average* which many people hold in their mind that hinders their ability to believe they're just as capable as wealthy people. If they do try something new, they simply give up easily—assuming that the road to wealth is too difficult for them, and that they—being poor little average types—obviously don't have what it takes.

It's like being stranded on an island with a small dinghy. You find a note left by previous castaways telling you there is land to the east. But you can't see it—you only have the anonymous words of an unknown predecessor to go on. What do you do? Do you sit on the shore and wait for a ship to carry you to what you perceive to be certain safety—not knowing when, or if, that would ever happen? Or would you get in the boat and start rowing?

To those who have traveled before you, the way seems obvious; they can't understand why you'd hesitate. But in your mind, you consider the 'what ifs'. What if the boat swamps? What if I lose my way? What if a shark eats me? You reason that the people who made it to land were lucky and had some kind of special help, or perhaps were smarter or more capable than you. Maybe they had something you don't—a map or a compass.

And after all, you're just an average person. How can *you* possibly accomplish such a feat? The fear grows in your mind and with it the expanse of water, however large it actually is, grows so huge in your mind that it may as well be an entire ocean. So you wait. Your entire life slips by while you hope for that ship to save you and take you to that place you've convinced yourself you can never reach on your own.

Many people live the lie of being average their whole lives. They convince themselves that they aren't special enough to live a wealthy life. But you have the same capacity to learn and achieve as any other person—perhaps even more so. But you must leave this notion of being 'average' behind. You have to stand up and say "I'm willing to do what it takes"—and *mean* it. If you choose to start this journey to wealth and riches, you have to decide, up front, to *finish*—not 'wait and see' if you can handle it. Commit to it. Focus on it. Visualize its end—the result you so desire. Only then can you break free from the *Attitude of Average* and rise above to claim that which is rightfully yours. In order to be wealthy you must be willing to get in the dinghy right now and start rowing!

How We Think

Before you can really begin to change the way you think, you first have to understand how your current thoughts and beliefs came to be. The mind is an incredibly powerful tool, yet few people ever stop and think about what creates their thought patterns, feelings and actions. Because of this, they become frustrated and confused by the results they experience; yet they feel powerless to change them.

A person's overall attitude is a composite of their thoughts, feelings and actions—not one or two, but all three working together. These thoughts, feelings and actions are a product of our conditioned behavior, which includes the environment in which we were raised, the education we were given and the people and events that have influenced our lives. We are all a product of our individual experiences, so each person's attitude is entirely unique. In order to understand how these ideas and actions have rooted themselves in our behavior, we need to understand how we learn.

Everything we know we have learned in four specific stages. Take the example of riding a bicycle. We start out in life not knowing or caring that bicycles even exist or that we might ever want to ride one. This stage is called *Unconscious Incompetence*. We don't know that we don't know. We go merrily though our day completely unaware that there might be a better way of transportation than our feet.

At some point during our childhood, we see others riding bicycles and the desire to ride one ourselves starts to blossom. This is the second stage of learning and is called *Conscious Incompetence*. Now we know we don't know how to ride a bicycle and we try to learn. As you know, it takes much concentration and effort to balance on a bicycle for the first time. We work hard and focus our efforts at staying erect until we are finally able to peddle without falling over. This third stage of learning is *called Conscious Competence*. We have proven we can ride the bicycle through focused concentration and effort.

Through repetition we become so good at riding that we no longer have to consciously think about staying upright on the bicycle. This is called *Unconscious Competence*—when we become so adept at performing a particular skill, we don't even think about how to do it anymore.

Once a skill is learned, the mind moves it into the sub-conscious and it becomes a part of us. We no longer need to think about it—we just do it. This same process is at work whether we are learning to drive a car, use a computer—*or create wealth*!

As humans, we think in pictures. If I told you to think of your car, your home or your family, you can see them instantly in your mind as clear images—snapshots of your life. But if I ask you to think of your mind, you have no picture. You might imagine a picture of your brain, but your brain is not your mind anymore than your knee is. Your mind exists in every cell of your body, but has no concrete physical location or manifestation.

As you and I think in pictures, it's hard to understand your mind and how it works unless we have an image or picture of the mind. To illustrate and explain this process we will be using the stick person example. I have used this in all of my programs worldwide for over 40 years and feel indebted to the man who originated it, back in 1934, Dr. Thurman Fleet of San Antonio, Texas.

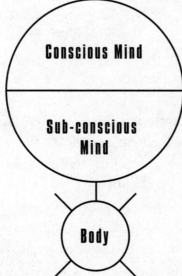

Conscious Mind

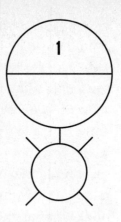

The top circle represents the mind or thoughts and the bottom circle represents your body or action. The mind is divided into the conscious and the sub-conscious. The conscious mind is the area where you receive all the input and experiences from the world around you. As new events and ideas are presented, your conscious mind has the ability to *accept or reject* any idea you choose. When ideas come to you from your surroundings, the conscious mind is the filter. This allows you to choose only those ideas and events you want to be emotionally involved with. The conscious mind is also where you create the dreams and goals that you want for your life.

Today, the best guess we can make is that, through the various kinds of media we all experience daily, each of us is bombarded with tens of thousands of images each and every day. Our conscious mind can effectively process less than a thousand of them.

The information age has made our lives more efficient, but it has also made them more complex. Every minute of every day, you are constantly choosing what your mind will process and be exposed to. But, like most people, you probably don't realize it's an active choice.

If you are constantly inundated with negative messages, you will choose negative thoughts and ideas. These are stored in your sub-conscious mind. The result? You become a negative person with negative ideas and opinions. If you want to think, feel and act more positively, you must guard your sub-conscious with your conscious mind. It is the gatekeeper. It allows you to choose what ideas you get emotionally involved with and what images you're exposed to over and over.

Sub-conscious Mind

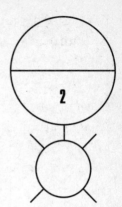

The sub-conscious mind is the "emotional" or "feeling" mind. The ancient Greeks called it "the heart of hearts." The sub-conscious mind only has one answer to all commands it receives from the conscious mind and that answer is "YES!" It accepts all ideas presented and incorporates them into your beliefs.

The sub-conscious mind has no ability to reject thoughts. This is why you need to use your conscious mind to monitor thoughts and ideas as you receive them—and close the gate when negative thoughts are approaching. If you worry about something happening, then the sub-conscious will move you in the direction of having that negative thing happen. Likewise, if you create a positive idea of how you want events to unfold or how you want to handle the unfortunate things that happen in your life, then the sub-conscious mind will internalize it and start working on the positive result.

Worrying and focusing on what you do not want takes just as much energy and time—if not more—than focusing on what you *do* want—and it works! You will always attract energy that you're in harmony with. If your energy is largely negative, then that's what you'll get back.

With this basic knowledge of how your mind operates, we can identify how negative emotions or feelings were implanted into your mind. You may have been raised with the belief that you can't get a good job without a good education. While this is completely untrue, repetition has planted it in your sub-conscious mind—so much so that you now only pursue jobs and opportunities that require exactly the level of education you have since you 'feel' unqualified to try for anything more.

Perhaps you experienced a failure at some point in your life.

By constantly replaying the emotions it created in your mind, you build an overwhelming fear of ever failing again. The sub-conscious mind has no ability to distinguish between what is actually happening and what you are remembering. Constantly focusing on past negative events creates an overwhelmingly negative attitude.

The good news is that by understanding how ideas are implanted in the mind, we are able to remedy their effects. We can counteract negative with positive. Every day focus on your positive achievements. Very quickly, you're diminishing the negative energy and attracting more positive events into your life. This is where visualization comes in. Remember, your mind can't tell if you are simply visualizing your new wealthy life or actually experiencing it, so it accepts your vision as fact. Through repetition, this idea of wealth becomes a part of your beliefs and positively affects your results. Remember believing is seeing? This is that simple concept made real.

I know this sounds quick and easy. Just focus on positive thoughts and focus on repeating them, and eventually they'll replace all the negative thoughts that you've built up in your sub-conscious over a lifetime. But there's more to it than that.

You can never underestimate the power of your mind and how hard it will try to hold onto what it already perceives to be real. This power can be all-consuming. The effort it takes to overcome a deeply-ingrained idea can be exhausting. You need to know that up front. Prepare for a fight. This is going to take stamina and determination. And understand this, you're quite capable of it.

The power of the sub-conscious mind to believe in something, even though your conscious mind knows it not to be correct, is an incredible phenomenon. Think of soldiers or accident victims who have lost a limb through a traumatic event. They can see and physically feel that the limb is no longer there, but the mind will continue to think otherwise. These patients will tell you that they can literally still 'feel' their limb attached. Sometimes, they will experience pain, or itching in the limb that has long since been severed. This can continue for months.

If it's that hard to convince your sub-conscious mind of something so physically obvious, imagine how hard it will be to remove ideas and thoughts that have been lodged in your mind since childhood. Your negative inclinations don't just disappear because you decided they should. It is an ongoing struggle and you have to commit to winning if you are to succeed.

X Throws Down the Gauntlet

Most of us live our lives without knowing—or caring—about the conditioning that governs our results. I call this conditioning the **X Factor.** And it's very important that you understand your conditioning controls your logic.

Think about those two young bicycle mechanics from Dayton, Ohio, Orville and Wilbur Wright. They thought illogically. You see, for centuries, it was logic that told us we could 0 fly. The Wright brothers thought outside of the box; their ideas were illogical. And, if you're going to win, you're going to have to be illogical. However, this conditioning and logic is not important until you attempt to do something that challenges your conditioning.

The X Factor can be any ingrained belief, from what weight you think you should be to how to raise your children. For our purposes, let's assume that X is the idea that you can never earn more than $100,000 per year. If you listen to those with a wealthy mindset, you may decide you want to earn $1 million per year. This new idea, the million dollars that is, is called the Y Factor. Now the war is on!

You'll entertain the new idea in your conscious mind at first. Maybe you'll visualize your new, wealthy life. The X factor will start gently. It will use logic, and try to convince you that maybe this new idea isn't right, or at least, not right for you. Your internal dialogue with X may go something like this:

"There's nothing wrong with how I'm living and I'm pretty happy. Why would I risk that?" And understand, your thinking is right. It's not going to get you to the million dollars, but it's right.

You may be able to push that argument aside. But if you do, the attack from X will get even more personal.

"Remember how hard you worked to get the job you have? What if this falls through and you can't get anything close to this? You know you need those benefits for your family."

X is relentless in its pursuit of what it believes. Even if you insist on believing that you will earn the $1 millon a year, X will keep chattering away in your mind, running through all the what-ifs and why-nots, over and over and over again. X wants to convince you that, no matter what you believe, there are far too many reasons it simply can't be done.

Every time you visualize a good reason why this will work, X will offer a rational, sensible reason why it won't. This is normal, and you should expect it. After all, X has been lounging around in your sub-conscious for a long time. X is comfortable there. Why would it want to move along? X wants you to do the same. It has invested a lifetime keeping you on the path you've always been on. Think about this—a path that's familiar and comfortable. In fact, X's very existence depends on you staying right where you are.

This is where persistence plays a key role. You have no chance against X unless you're willing to constantly reinforce this new idea. Unfortunately, your X Factor still has a secret weapon: Fear.

When fear enters the picture, logic leaves. Think about that. When fear enters the picture, logic leaves. It really doesn't matter how irrational or unfounded the fear may be; fear allows doubt and uncertainty to flood your mind and overcome this new idea that you've been so sure about. Let's assume that you've decided to start a new business and have just started your first bit of marketing—and nothing happens. Even though you know on a conscious level that it takes time, on a sub-conscious level your insecurities are playing havoc with your state of mind. "What if no one ever responds?" "What if this is all a mistake?" "What if I fall flat on my face?"

No matter how much you think you want to try and develop a new mindset of wealth, your old beliefs about money will constantly try to wear down your resolve. If you make the mistake of giving in to this fear and worrying about it constantly, it will only serve to bring about your worst-case scenario.

Let me share a story with you about a woman named Sally. She decided to quit her job to become a writer. She was already well on her way. She was producing income from her writing before she quit her corporate marketing job. She tells of her own battle with X:

"I looked forward to quitting my day job for years. I'd always dreamed of writing for a living, and over the past four years had built my freelance business up to a substantial level. The week that I finally quit I was exhilarated and ready to start my new life.

That feeling lasted about seven days. The beginning of my second week working from home I was consumed by a feeling of fear that I can't even explain. I'd already proven to myself that I could do this and I had enough jobs lined up to last several months. But still the what-ifs would not leave me alone. What if the jobs dried up? What if I missed my deadlines? What if my house burned down with all my research files! Most of them weren't even rational or logical but they kept me awake at night worrying.

After a couple of weeks drowning in this fear, I realized that I'd hardly worked at all. I'd always thought that I could never really make a living writing and now, due to my negative mindset and constant worry, it was coming true! I quickly refocused my mind on the positive vision I'd had of creating a career I loved and refused to allow my mind to dwell on the fear.

Sure enough, the fear subsided but that doesn't mean it has never reared its head since. It has, but now I know to immediately focus on the positive and refuse to allow it to distract me from what I really want for my life."

You see, as Sally found out, your sub-conscious will accommodate any thought that you entertain. If those thoughts are negative, it will provide even more negative reinforcement. When you reduce your efforts, or quit because of fear, you give yourself a lot of good reasons for the decision you made—"It's too difficult," "I'm in over my head," "I don't have the skills for this." But fear is rarely one of them.

Fear is actually the trigger for this mental rebellion. Fear provides an avenue for all the worries and concerns you've ever had to come pouring through. For many of us, it's almost impossible to resist for any period of time.

When you introduce and implement a new idea or way of thinking, power comes from your belief that this new idea is right and good. If fear takes over, it closes off your channel to this power. It internalizes your problem. Fear can keep you from logically working out the next step that you need to find the solution you require. It shuts you down. It helps you make an excuse to give up.

Take starting a new business. Fear can rob you of the ability to see what is really going on in the marketplace. It can keep you from seeing additional opportunities. It can alter the way you perceive your current results. If fear dominates your mindset, you could easily assume that you're a bad businessperson or that your product won't work for the market you had envisioned.

But the truth could very well be that you are simply approaching the market from the wrong angle, and your marketing could be more effective.

You need to learn to push the fear aside so you can see it for what it really is. If you can master fear, you can look for solutions and not waste energy worrying. When you're dealing with **X and Y Factors**, your channel of power is either open or closed. Only by constantly reinforcing the new ideas, and practicing new actions that support that idea, will you be able to keep this channel to power open. It is what gives you the tools to overcome your old way of thinking.

Remember, you have the ability to reject the fear your **X Factor** tortures you with. You have the *choice* not to dwell on the what-ifs. You don't have to give into fear. I have a good friend of mine, Melonie Brown. She's writing a book, "Let Fear Fail." That's a great title and it's going to be a great book.

You choose to *reject* that fear by allowing yourself to become emotionally involved with the Y Factor and all the good it's going to bring into your life.

Any new idea or thought process you introduce has to, with your help, grow strong—strong enough to overpower the old ideas deep-set in your mind. Those old thoughts don't just magically disappear. It is a fight and a struggle. And once you've accepted the new idea and truly believe in it, you must remain vigilant. Keep that new idea strong and the negative ideas at bay, because given the chance, they'll try their best to come home. Make no mistake about it. Close the door; don't let them in.

Many people express their wants and desires as a wish. This is why: They hope that their lives will change but they have not made the commitment to make that happen. They want it to be easy—a fantasy that comes true with the wave of a magic wand. And of course, it doesn't. They quickly fall back into old habits and never move toward what they say they want.

Eventually, they convince themselves it was just a pipe dream anyway, and that it never could have happened. The sad part is that it absolutely could have! They could have had everything their hearts desired, but they didn't commit to the new idea. Thus, the old negative thoughts weren't even disturbed. They didn't even need to make an argument. And if you make it that easy on your X Factor, I promise you, you'll get the same results. And I know you don't want to go through life saying "I could have been a millionaire."

The thoughts, habits and attitude of the life you have been living up to now have produced the results you now live with. These new ideas are a struggle to implement, but they will be what produce the life you dream of as long as you can stay focused. If you do, the new ideas will find a permanent home in your mind. This is the best result you can hope for. As the new idea becomes stronger, you'll see the results manifest themselves in your life. Over time, it becomes your new paradigm or belief. If you can go from making $100,000 per year to $1 million then why not $10 million? Or $100 million? Why not?

I often tell people to start with the idea that they can turn their yearly income into a monthly income. This gives them an exact dollar figure to work with in their mind. It's important to be precise. If you start with an idea that you just 'want more money,' that doesn't give you a concept that you can become emotionally involved with. Five dollars is 'more money;' it's just too vague. Once you have an amount—let's work with $1 million—then you are able to start searching for ways to make that figure a reality.

Buy yourself a small calculator like I have and carry it with you all the time like I do. When I find myself with some extra time, waiting in an airport or flying from one place to the next, I will often take out this little calculator and start working out how I will make my next million dollars. The first thing I do is to punch the total amount I want to earn into the calculator—$1,000,000.

Henry Ford said if you want to make a big job easy, break it into small parts. I take what he said literally. I divide the million by 12—that's for 12 months—meaning, I'm going to give myself a year to do this. One million divided by 12 is $83,333. That's how much I have to earn every month, but that's still a pretty big number. So let's reduce if further. We'll divide the $83,333 by 4.3— since there are 4.3 weeks per month. Our new number is $19,380. So, that's how much I have to earn every week.

Now, for a brand new idea, that still sounds like quite a lot. So, I think I'll break my week into two parts: Monday to Wednesday; Thursday to Sunday. I'll divide $19,380 by 2, which takes the number down to $9,690. You may be thinking, 'wow, I've got to earn $9,690 between Monday and Wednesday and then again, between Thursday and Sunday ... and I've got to do that every week, all year long!'

I think we'd better apply Ford's method to this once again.

Divide $9,690 by 86. Now, you're probably wondering, why 86? I just arbitrarily picked that number ... I could have picked 74, but I didn't, I picked 86. Stay with me—there's a good idea here. The answer to that is $112.67. Let that stick in your mind, $112.67.

Now let me ask you a question. If I could show you how to earn, one thousand, one hundred and twelve dollars and sixty seven cents twice a week, every week, with very little effort, would you give me the $112.67 and keep the thousand? You're probably saying, sure I'd do that. I have gone through this calculation in numerous seminars and I've never had a person say no, they wouldn't do it.

Think of what I'm asking you. I'm going to show you how to earn an extra thousand dollars twice a week and $112.67 on top of the thousand, and because I'm originating the idea, it's my intellectual property, you're going to give me a fraction of what you earn, $112.67 twice a week. Stay with me. Now, I don't have to figure out how to earn one million dollars any more, I just have to think of an idea that will enable you to earn $1,112.67 twice a week and when I've got that figured out, I don't think I'll have any trouble getting 85 other people willing to do what you're willing to do.

Now, you see, earning money isn't difficult if you think. The problem with most people is they don't think. They've tricked themselves into believing that mental activity is thinking. That idea was a bit of a shock to me the first time I'd heard it. I was listening to Earl Nightingale's recording, The Strangest Secret, where he quoted the late Dr. Albert Schweitzer who was being interviewed by a reporter as he got off the plane. The reporter asked the good doctor, what was the problem with people today? He thought about it for a moment and said, "People simply don't think." And, if you observe people as I have, ever since I first heard that recording many years ago, you will very likely find what I have found—that most people would never say what they were saying if they were thinking and they would most certainly never do what they are doing if they were thinking. Dr. Schweitzer was right—people just don't think. When you begin thinking, which is the highest function of which you are capable, your whole life will change.

Let me give you some other examples, should you doubt that anyone—from any walk of life—can create this passive income. These are a few occupations that are very common, and I have several suggestions for creating passive income with each one of them:

Exercise Instructor: Create a unique exercise regime and write a book about it. Produce DVDs of this regime for various levels of students. Offer training seminars for other instructors to learn to teach your system. Create a diet workbook that goes along with the exercise regime.

Teacher: Create DVDs to tutor children in various subjects and sell companion workbooks. Write a book for parents on how to help their children learn better. If you are a coach, you can sell DVDs and books that help athletes train. If you are a music teacher, you can sell items that teach people to play the guitar or piano.

Contractor: Create DVDs to help people understand the basics of remodeling their homes. Write a book about how to find a good contractor and work with them effectively to build a dream home.

And finally, if you're a **Customer Service Representative:** Create a how-to handbook on basic customer service skills to sell to employers. Create a DVD for consumers on how to work with customer service representatives to resolve problems effectively.

You see, from these examples that I have just shared with you, you can use the skills you have right now to create passive income. It doesn't matter what those skills are as long as they provide value in some way. Don't sit and think that you have nothing to offer!

Not only do you have the opportunity to create the life you dream of, you also have the ability to positively affect the lives of others. It is this desire and passion to get your knowledge out to those who can benefit from it that creates the passion necessary to put everything in motion. I experienced this passion as a young man in my 20s. Once I discovered the path to wealth, I wanted to tell everyone I knew! I wanted to share these ideas and shout it from the mountaintops—and for the past 40 years that's exactly what I've done.

Now, you can begin your own journey of discovery and wealth. Each is different and your path will be as unique as you are—but it is there. Your road to wealth already exists if you have the courage to find it.

Now, for a quick review of Chapter 2.

Chapter 2 REVIEW

- Find what you are passionate about and use that passion to fulfill your dreams.
- Let go of the Attitude of Average.
- Your attitude is a combination of your thoughts, feelings and actions.
- You must guard what your mind is exposed to.
- Don't underestimate the power of your ingrained belief systems.
- You must persist in creating new thoughts to prevent falling back into your old negative patterns.
- Believe that you have the skills right now to provide value and create passive income.
- Don't wait—decide to get in your dinghy and start rowing!
- Investigate multiple sources of income. Let me give you an example. Go to www.BobProctorMoney.com/CC —that's an organization of people from all around the world who have come together to help each other set up multiple sources of income.

Chapter 3

Don't Be an Extra in Your Own Movie

I've always been fascinated with the study of human potential. You simply cannot tell what someone might be able to achieve simply by looking at them. Some achieve extraordinary feats through almost unimaginable adversity. Some suffer terrible tragedies, but emerge as competent, confident human beings. And some seem to be denied any possible advantage in life and yet emerge as significant symbols of triumph. Think of Helen Keller: Blind and deaf before she was two years old, she went on to become an articulate champion of disabled people's rights. Joan of Arc became a leader of men in an era when women who challenged authority were burned at the stake. Bill Gates was a college dropout, but he changed the world and helped usher in the computer era. John F. Kennedy galvanized a nation and thrust them into the Space Age with nothing but a vision of landing a man on the moon. Martin Luther King inspired a social revolution of non-violent change in a segment of the population that had been oppressed for generations.

What would you say if I told you that you have exactly the same potential to change your world as any of these great people? You'd find that hard to believe, I'm sure. But if I was to take you through the streets of almost any city in the world and point out a homeless person, would you think you had more potential to achieve than they do? You probably would. If I pointed out one of your coworkers, would you consider your potential at least equal to if not better than theirs? What if we were in New York and saw Donald Trump speed past in his limo? Would you think that you have the same potential as him? Probably not.

Why?

It's simple conditioning. We tend to judge what a person can or cannot accomplish by their current results. If their current results are poor, then we assume that they will always be poor. If your current results are what you consider average, then it's easy to project that you'll always be average. If you see someone incredibly wealthy, then of course we'll expect that they have the most potential of all, because their results are so great.

We play this comparison game in our heads, and decide where we fit. But as I've already discussed, your present results have absolutely nothing to do with your future. *They are completely irrelevant.* The perception that you are less than anyone else who walks this planet is ridiculous. You are equal to any other person on this earth, and they are equal to you. There is no shortage of success or wealth. There is an abundant supply to go around. This means *that every single person has the same potential.* The only differences are the ones we perceive in our mind.

This is especially noticeable in children. When young children start school, they believe what they are told. If they are told they are slow or stupid, they believe it—even though it's completely untrue. If they're told they're brilliant and gifted, then they believe that—and their performance rises to meet that expectation.

What you believe about yourself and your potential stems from a hodgepodge of experiences and statements that you took in as a child. You had no choice but to believe them. Your conscious mind was untrained and unable to filter them and your sub-conscious accepted them as fact. Unless you specifically try to change those beliefs, you will continue believing them no matter what. In order to achieve great things, you have to believe you have the same potential that everyone else has—and you must commit to developing that potential.

Be an Original

As Ralph Waldo Emerson once said, "There will come a time in every person's education when they'll realize that envy is ignorance and imitation is suicide." I really think of this directly in terms of anyone who wants to live a wealthy life.

Why? Well, one of the biggest things you have to accept is that you have the same potential as anyone else. And if that's the case, what reason could you have to envy anyone else? If your potential is the same, then your results could also be the same.

When I started studying how wealth was achieved, this is one of the first lessons I learned. If you want the same results as wealthy people, then you must take action to create those results yourself!

Emerson also says that "imitation is suicide." And it's true. Every single person who achieves great wealth does so in a slightly different manner. They are their own person with their own passions—just like you are. You can't just duplicate someone else's actions and expect to achieve their success, because the path to wealth is passion, and passion, as we know, is as unique and individual as each person on this planet. This is why you need to find *your own personal passion* to create wealth.

I hope this comes as something of a relief. Just think: you don't have to be a real estate magnate like Donald Trump to achieve wealth—or an international public speaker, like me. I know this first hand. I know of many people who have tried to do exactly what I'm doing. And you know what? I'm never threatened by it. In fact, I'm happy to give them every little detail of how I do what I do.

Often, after a few months of trying, they come back (sometimes a little annoyed) and want to know what I've left out. They can't understand why their results have been so poor when they have been imitating exactly what I do. But as we've just pointed out, what's missing is not something I've left out—it's something in them. No matter how closely they imitate me, they can't create the passion I have for what I do. This is why you have to find your own passion—that one thing that inspires you to leap out of bed each day eager for the challenge.

Knowing that you have the potential to create any life that you choose, how can you justify trading time for money now to live the life you really want in the future? How can you say that your time is worth $20 per hour or even $40 per hour? Your time is worth a limitless amount! By putting an artificial dollar amount on it you become the architect of your own failure. Thousands of people around the world can understand and agree that they have potential, but how many actually take charge of their lives and do something about it? I'm sad to say, very few.

Most of us can grasp the possibility of change in our mind, but that's very different than committing to it—committing to overcome your programming and beliefs that have been drilled into you your entire life. But unless you do, it will remain only that: A possibility, and unrealized potential. This puts you back where you started: The excitement soon turns to apathy and apathy sends you to the same old job every day.

Your life reassumes its drudgerous routine. It convinces you that you need some downtime, that you should spend that time plopped in front of the television watching pain, suffering and negative ideas for hours on end. It drives you to apathy. And apathy is like a sadistic drug which deadens your mind from wanting more. It convinces you that you're okay as you are. It is the friend of the average, and as such, the mortal enemy of true wealth.

The Law of Attraction

Over the past few years the *Law of Attraction* has gotten a lot of attention. And why not? The idea that you can attract what you want into your life is, well, pretty attractive, isn't it?

However, you need to understand that the *Law of Attraction* is—and always has been—at work in your life. You just didn't know it. The basic explanation of this law is that everything in our lives is drawn to us by our thoughts. The *Law of Attraction* is always at work: Everything that happens to us—good, bad or indifferent—we have brought on ourselves, even though we may never understand why.

I say this because often, I'm asked why bad events or catastrophes occur. To be honest, I don't know. But I can tell you that you have the ability to attract good and positive events into your life if you choose to. We have already touched on the power that your thoughts and beliefs have and how they affect your mind. The *Law of Attraction* deals with how these thoughts affect the world around you.

It may sound simple. But it demands a heavy dose of personal responsibility. To attract the positive results and wealth that you desire, you must first understand and accept that all that has happened to you so far, you have also attracted—that they are your responsibility, no-one else's.

Few people are willing to do this. More commonly, they prefer to blame others, or fate, while pushing aside the idea that their own thoughts and beliefs are responsible for their current results.

The *Law of Attraction* is actually a sub-law of the *Law of Vibration* which says that everything is energy, and that energy is constantly moving, or vibrating. This is true for physical objects, which are vibrating on an atomic level, as well as for the energy created by your thoughts. Every time you think something, you're putting energy in motion. Energy attracts more energy of the same kind. Thus, positive thoughts are magnets for more positive energy, while negative thoughts, well, I don't have to spell that out now, do I?

It's important to keep this in mind, because the *Law of Attraction* doesn't have the ability to discriminate—it can create good or bad results in equal measure. It doesn't have an opinion; it simply gives you what you focus on. And this is important: it doesn't give you what you say you want—*but what you focus on.*

Remember earlier, where I told you that you should focus on what you want to happen rather than focusing and worrying about something negative like all the bills you have to pay? This is important because of the *Law of Attraction*. The more you worry about these sorts of things, the more you focus on your fear that you will not make enough money. And that's likely to take you exactly where you don't want to go...towards insolvency, or worse.

By focusing on creating more wealth, you will attract the solutions and answers that will provide more income. Then, what you've practiced—not worrying about how to pay those bills—will simply become a reality.

So clearly, we want to use the *Law of Attraction* in our favor, not our detriment. But first, we need to take a good hard look at our present results. I'm not saying you should feel bad about them especially since we know that feeling bad about something will just attract more of the same. No, you should do the best you can to take an objective look. Ask yourself what kind of friends you currently have. What kind of coworkers? How do you feel about your level of income? How is your business going?

As the answers to these questions flash through your mind, write them down. And make sure you write the first answer that pops into your head—not the sugar-coated one that rationalized and justifies the results that you don't really want.

Then, as you look at your list, realize that these ideas are responsible for programming your results in life thus far. Your every result in life is magnetized to a specific thought and belief that you have. Your initial thoughts are a reflection of your subconscious beliefs, and that's what attracted this current reality into your life.

It's quite common for people who try this exercise to find that they dislike the thoughts and beliefs they uncover. But take a step back. Recognize that they are merely a reflection of what has been in your life, and that you have the ability to change them if you want to. This is why I spend so much time talking about how to change your mindset and move positive thoughts into your subconscious—they are what the *Law of Attraction* works from.

Unfortunately, many people who read this information about the *Law of Attraction* still get the very same results in their life. No matter how many times I speak to audiences or share my thoughts with them through my books, audio products or coaching programs, many people still exhibit the same results year after year—even decade after decade! It's a sad and terrible thing to witness. I know they understand what I've told them. They know intellectually that this makes good logical sense. They've probably heard it repeatedly not only from me, but from many others who understand its power. But their results indicate that they really never understood it to the point of incorporating it into their lives.

Why? Well, often, people stop at that first step—looking at their results. Taking responsibility for a life you don't like, and acknowledging that you created it, can be heartbreaking. . Few people have the strength it takes to work though that old programming. It hurts to look at a disappointing result and accept blame for it. So they set it aside and avoid the issue. But what they don't consider is that they're are still invoking the *Law of Attraction*—you can't turn it off; one way or another, it's always working. And by pushing their disappointment aside, they're fuelling the *Law of Attraction* in a negative and destructive way.

You have to commit to being one of those willing to accept your situation as self-created, and you have to commit to use the *Law of Attraction* to help you in your pursuit of wealth. After you take stock of where you are and take responsibility for what has produced your results, you're ready to move forward.

Maybe you've already tried to choose the ideas and thoughts that would bring about a positive vibration but you haven't made any progress yet. Be very aware of outside influences: Every person you spend time with, everything you see and hear on television, and even random, overheard conversations—they all have their own vibration. If you associate with people who have a negative vibration, it's hard for you to constantly choose positive ideas.

If you have a friend or family member who is constantly spouting a litany of negative thoughts—complaining about his or her job, relationships, lack of money—then it's going to hamper your ability to project the positive. How many times have you noticed that, after being with this person, you feel physically drained? The fact is, you are—they've sucked your positive energy right out of you!

You can correct this, but it means staying away from negative people like this. Of course, we can't always choose our business associates—and never our families!—so simply avoiding them it isn't always practical. So the best way to protect yourself is to refuse to become emotionally involved in their negative energy. Refuse to commiserate. Don't get dragged down with them. That can lessen the impact of their negative thoughts, and allows your positive ones to shine through!

Outside influences will always threaten to mix their opposing or discordant energies with your own. If you allow yourself to get emotionally involved in these influences, then the wealthy life that you want will evaporate into thin air. You must be steadfast to change your results and incredibly determined to guard your mind from negative thoughts.

Go back to the first questions I asked about your life and income. Analyze your responses. Where did those ideas originate? From something you heard or experienced in childhood? Are they the words of a teacher, parent or other influential person? Are they the result of an encounter with a boss, spouse or former spouse? Do you want to continue to allow their thoughts and ideas to control your results?

At some point, even small children will rebel against the instructions they are given by adults. I saw this happen at a restaurant with a little girl who was being told to eat some type of vegetable she obviously didn't like. Each time her mother would try to get her to take a bite, the little girl's response was the same. She crossed her arms and gritted her teeth and said, "You're not the boss of me!"

When you think of the outside influences that have rattled around in your mind for most of your life, this is a great response: *"You're not the boss of me!"* You can choose to change and reject those old ideas, but it takes a stubborn, single-minded will and determination to make it happen. Just like that little girl who was determined not to allow one bite past her gritted teeth, you must have that kind of tenacity to change your thoughts.

Until you recognize where the thoughts that created your results came from and resolve to change those thoughts, you won't make much progress toward a wealthy mindset. Once you understand them, it then takes a strong commitment to see this change through. This takes much more than the occasional wish or New Year's resolution. It takes firm commitment. But this commitment is just the starting point.

On Your Mark, Get Set . . .

You're now at the starting gate and ready to run. But you need to know where the finish line is. You must have a very clear picture in your mind of where you are going. If you don't, your vibration will have no clue what to focus on. I've seen this happen many times: When the end result is not clear, the results are lack lustre at best.

This can lead you to make the mistake of thinking that none of these ideas are working. At worst, this can justify your retreat to a life less than extraordinary: You think you're doing everything right, but the wealth you expected isn't streaming in. In fact, there's not even a trickle! So you accept failure and contemplate quitting altogether.

But wait! You do have commitment, you have the intelligence and you've learned to focus on the positive. So what gives? You haven't created a really concrete idea of what you want. It's like running with no finish line—you just keep going and going—eventually you wear out! Does this describe your current situation? Then go back to the first technique I talked about in Chapter 1. Visualize what you want in as much detail as you possibly can.

Write down—in the present tense—what your business will be like when you reach your goal. You might say, "I am so happy and grateful now that I earn thousands every day providing value and quality to my clients." Keep the wording positive and focus on what you want—not what you don't. You might say, "I easily earn more than enough to pay my expenses and provide for my family," not "I don't run out of money before the end of the month."

As you imagine your new wealthy life, imagine the home you live in. Picture this as if you are actually walking through the house giving someone a tour. Notice the quality woods and beautifully stained floors, the plush rugs and granite counters. Notice every detail, from the exotic fresh flower arrangement on the table to the crystal in the cabinet.

Now do the same with your business. If you imagine working from home, then picture a home office that has everything you need within easy reach. Imagine being able to walk out to your garden for a coffee break or pick up your children from school. This type of intricate detail allows you to become emotionally involved with the new image that you're now creating.

Revisit this image in your mind on a daily basis. This is extremely important: Each day imagine some new scenario that is part of this end result—perhaps an international business meeting where you discuss taking your concept worldwide or the purchase of a new vacation home on a Caribbean island. Imagine your toes in the sand as you see, hear and smell the waves bubble onto the beautiful shore.

You can even include others in your image—your parents, maybe. Imagine buying them a dream home or taking them on a once in a lifetime cruise. Think of how it will feel to use your new wealth to help others. Write those feelings down and hold tight to that emotion. Writing descriptions of the images causes you to think and as you think you create new and more intricate images. These stir emotion and emotions are expressed in action. Action sets up a reaction and thus alters your circumstance, environment and the conditions in your life. This isn't some miraculous spell. It's the *Law of Attraction*.

The more you focus on building this new image, the faster your actual results will begin to parallel that image. The more attention and focus you give that new, vibrant picture, the faster the expansion of energetic vibration. This energy is highly charged and vibrates at an increasing rate. The increase amplifies your thoughts bringing results that are better, faster and more complete. Every time you entertain this image you're setting energy into motion. You're impressing a picture on the subjective mind and creating new recognition and emotion. That vibration moves into action—it can't help itself. But now the action is creating the *results you want*, not the ones you don't.

It is important to understand that this doesn't happen

overnight. I tell people to fully expect to do this for at least 30 days before anything happens, and even then it may be something small. Of course, I frequently hear of people who try this for just a few days and immediately experience results. That could be the case for you, but understand that usually it takes time. This has nothing to do with luck but it does have to do with awareness. Every person has different programming and a different amount or potency of old beliefs to overcome before they can gain an awareness of wealth and a wealthy mindset. For this reason, everyone's path and experience is different—and so too is how long the shift takes to manifest.

The good news is that once you start building this new image, you don't want to go back—you don't want to settle for less than your mind is now imagining and believing. Your awareness has already expanded to this new place and you have created an emotional attachment to it. This encourages you to continue to press forward. So keep that image firmly in your mind and don't allow yourself to get discouraged. Remember how hard the mind holds on to ideas. As with a severed limb, it often takes time to convince the mind that things have changed!

Old beliefs are very strong. This is because they are a combination of memories, pain and emotion, as well as pictures of people, places and events. It's not just a negative habit of thought—these beliefs are multilayered and complex. They are not just single thoughts, but part of an entire group of habits that support those thoughts. This is why "think positive" programs don't work. You can't apply a one-dimensional solution to a multidimensional problem. You must use all the techniques I've outlined—just one or two won't work. They must be used together.

Even though the entire process might take longer than you want or think it should, it will happen. I guarantee you will begin to notice changes in your life and your ability to attract opportunities for wealth. As you begin to see small differences and changes here and there, you'll get even more emotionally involved in making this reality happen. And that's when you need to keep your enthusiasm rolling and renew your commitment to creating a wealthy mindset.

As with any goal in life that you truly want to achieve, at first you'll need to invest a great deal of personal resources, including time. But you already know this. I bet you can think of one or two accomplishments in your life that required a great deal of time and focused, energetic commitment. When you first started, it wasn't comfortable at all—in fact, it might have even been painful. You probably had to give up other things to keep your commitment. But you wanted this thing more. You yearned for it. So you kept going.

This is known as disciplined repetition. Eventually, you're so focused on your goal that you stop thinking about what you are giving up to pursue it. It has become the priority in your life and you're determined to achieve it.

Think about your daily routine right now. There are segments of time you've set aside to things that you once held to be important. Are they as important as developing a new, wealthy mindset? If your answer is yes, how likely are you to devote the necessary time to your new life? If you're really committed to changing for the better, you'll shift your priorities and devote the time you need.

With every specific new image or new positive belief that you incorporate, you'll notice other areas of your life improve as well. They benefit from the positive energy spilling over. You'll also start to inspire others who witness your transformation—especially those who are close to you. The way you live your new life will affect positive change for you, but your family and future generations will benefit too as they learn from your example. This is another great reason not to put it off one day longer!

I often hear people talk about "someday" as the place where

their dreams will finally come true. But I know that "someday" is a killer of possibilities and a destroyer of dreams. To delay is to miss out on all life has to offer you. The decisions you make right now will determine your future results. If you delay the change you need to effect, and that becomes your way of being, then I can assure you "someday" will never come.

Fate and Her Sister Destiny

The idea that your life is predetermined and can't be changed is a common theological debate. Of course, if this was true, we wouldn't have the power to choose, but we do. People often use the ideas of fate or destiny to absolve themselves of responsibility for their results. It's easier to blame an outside entity or force than to shoulder the blame yourself. Most people understand "fate" as something static—as if there were a message written in the stars that said, "This is the way it's going to be and it's not up to me." No wonder a passive life develops from this attitude, where people wait for their fate to find them and just "happen." It is much like waiting on that ship to take you off the island.

Many people live their lives thinking that fate will come along and anoint them with wealth if it's meant to be. Too often, years go by before they realize that in all this time they haven't experienced anything—they've virtually slept through their days in a monotonous routine of work, lunch, dinner, occasional entertainment, television and rest. Each day is the same boring routine, until the days become months and the months stretch into years.

These same individuals often struggle to make ends meet. As they sit and wait for something—anything—to happen, it's easy for them to adopt the mindset that wealth is something that's "just not meant to be" for them. They give up on bettering their circumstances and their standard of living spirals downward.

They are pushed around by events they have attracted with their negative attitude and their lives become progressively worse.

These people are truly locked within their *Prison of Perception*. One movie that I particularly like is called *The Shawshank Redemption*. An idea that this movie works with is the notion that prisoners, over time, become "institutionalized." This means that they come to accept their jail cell and prison life as their home; that prison is the only place they belong. Their dreams of freedom die. If they're released, they'll commit a crime just to be sent back. The prisoners become so use to their limited life within the walls of their cell that the outside world seems foreign and frightening.

People who have chosen to live within the limits of their old beliefs experience something very similar. This is most evident when someone presents a new and exciting possibility or opportunity to them. They will immediately reject the idea and get as far away as possible. If they accept that they might have a better life, or that their current situation is their responsibility, then they will not be able to go on as they always have.

Many people live in a mental prison as strong and confining as those who are behind bars. They have all the freedom in the world but they exercise none of it because they are afraid to believe, like a prisoner, that a better life *can* be theirs. They prefer to believe that it is not possible for them and that some outside force, like fate, is responsible.

Why? Because it takes courage to change your life. It takes effort and commitment to break the old patterns, change old habits and rebuild your thought process. It is easier to stay where you are, blame fate and tell yourself, "No, this is too hard. Who am I to think that I can make it happen? What if I fail? Right now, I have *something*. Maybe it isn't the life that I want or even one that I like—but it's mine and I don't want to lose what I have."

The idea of destiny isn't much different. How can anyone be destined for wealth or riches? It almost sounds like a birthright that is bestowed on the chosen few with a wave of a magic wand. However, wealthy people, those that preserve and grow their wealth, do so through working at it not by having it bestowed upon them by destiny.

You can see the truth of this with people who inherit wealth. Often, if wealth is handed to them and they've never known how to work at it, they merely squander their money on useless frivolity. They haven't gained a mindset of wealth—that's definitely not inherited!

Wealth will only come through learning how to think wealthy and applying the principles of attraction and positive energy. Gary Player, one of the best golfers of his time, once said: "The harder I work, the luckier I am." He knew that there was no magic or fate involved no matter how it may look to outside observers.

Someone who seems to accumulate wealth easily isn't lucky. They don't have fate on their side and they are not destined to be wealthy. They have merely developed the mindset and skill to make it *look* easy. Commit yourself right now to doing what it takes to develop a wealthy mindset for yourself and your efforts will bring the reward you seek.

We are each born with an equal measure of potential and wealth is the birthright of every single person. This does not diminish over time so no matter how old you are you can still tap into the infinite abundance that has always been yours. In fact, the more experiences you have had, the more value you can provide for others. I've known numerous people who have had several careers in their lives and this is a great resource to draw from when you are looking for ways to create value.

Nothing happens by chance or accident. The life you have led up to this point may not have produced the results you would like, but it can provide the seeds for your future as you search for your passion. You don't stumble through life hoping for the best. You can actively plan your future and visualize it.

Many people are surprised at the sense of empowerment they get once they accept responsibility and stop blaming fate and destiny for their results. They have spent so much time floating through their lives with no notion of where they want to go, visualizing that finish line is a powerful new sensation. Your life is completely within your control and the events that you choose to experience are what make you a unique individual. Your new sense of empowerment will allow you to enjoy those events more fully as you realize that you created them and now have the ability to create and bring about whatever you desire.

Chapter 3 REVIEW

- Stop comparing your results to the results of others.
- Your present results are completely irrelevant.
- Be unique—you can't imitate someone else's passion.
- Your time is invaluable.
- Apathy is the friend of the average and the enemy of true wealth.
- You must accept responsibility for your current results.
- The *Law of Attraction* does not judge—it gives you what you focus on.
- It takes great courage to change your life.

Chapter 4

Purpose, Vision, Goals

Wealthy people do what they love. I've said this over and over. Why? Because it's true. If you plan to join their ranks, you have to embrace what you love. As a unique individual, you have specific talents and abilities that no one else has. You also have your own likes and dislikes.

As you go through life, you try new things. You find there are some things that you are drawn to and at which you excel. This begins in childhood when each of us starts to differentiate ourselves from others. Some children are drawn to music where others may have an affinity for art. Still others may prefer to tell stories, while their classmates are fascinated by numbers. You were born with a unique set of gifts and talents. They're genetically implanted into your mind. These talents are discovered as you grow and move through life.

Your purpose in life will be drawn from this unique set of gifts and talents This purpose is the thing that sets you apart and justifies your reason for being. It is something as unique as a fingerprint that only you can discover. Think about it: The exact mix of talent and purpose that defines who you are has never existed in anyone else that has ever lived! New and innovative ideas spring forth from this resource in you. It is why we are still making new discoveries each and every day.

Your purpose is much like an internal guidance system. It directs your actions and thoughts and focuses them to create the life you desire. But not everyone knows their purpose. They may never have thought about it or considered that they have a purpose at all! But they do. If you do not know your purpose, you can feel like you're living a "hit and run" life. You hurry from point to point trying one thing and then another in an attempt to make your life what you want it to be. But without a purpose to guide you in your efforts, you're just spinning your wheels and tiring out. You aren't really getting anywhere.

You may feel stuck, bored and disconnected from what is going on in your life. The cure for this disconnectedness is to discover your purpose. You should start by looking at those activities you love and are good at. But this doesn't mean that you should discount or disqualify any of your talents. How often have you heard someone say, "Well, I'm an artist but I need to get a real job," or "I like to sing but it's just a hobby," or "I like to talk to people but you can't make a living doing that."

You'll frequently hear people tell you what they love only to have them disclaim their gifts as hobbies or worthless diversions. It's not true. You can create wealth from virtually anything! It's a mistake to assume that, simply because you enjoy something, it can't also be your livelihood. Once you define exactly what your purpose is you won't even have to try to figure out how to make money. The ideas will flow freely as if someone was whispering in your ear. Everything will come together beautifully.

We talked earlier about imitation being deadly because you can't imitate someone else's passion. The secret to finding your purpose is to follow *your* passion. Look at the activities that you would do whether you got paid or not. Think about those times where you were so wrapped up in something that hours flew by almost unnoticed. This is where you look to find your purpose. And you shouldn't have to look hard. The answer will pop into your mind almost immediately. The problem occurs when you immediately discount the ideas because of your old beliefs. One of those is the myth that you can't earn a living doing what you love. Force yourself not to disqualify any ideas that come to mind. Make a list of every thought that comes to you as you search for those things you enjoy.

Another belief or reason that might cause you to squelch valid ideas is being on a track already. You've already got a significant amount of time, money and energy invested in the direction you are going now, you tell yourself. How can I change that? If you consider that your current path might not be your true purpose, you realize that it might require a complete change of occupation. This can be very difficult if you have worked very hard to get the education and experience required for your current occupation. It often seems almost wasteful to "throw it all away."

Think about that for a moment. What does it mean to throw it all away? Does it mean that you will never again benefit from anything that you have learned so far? No. Does it mean that you will be worse off than you are right now? No. Does it mean that you are giving up? No. Does it mean that life will change? Yes. It is the change that is most frightening. The idea that you might change professions midstream is a major shift in your life's expectations. However, you must view change as just that—a major shift. You are switching courses but that doesn't mean that your education and professional experiences won't benefit you. It also doesn't mean that you will be destitute or worse off. I ask you, is it better to go work at something that you love and are passionate about or to stay in a job you barely tolerate because you feel obligated?

Purpose Is the Why

When you discover that one idea that sparks the passion within you, you'll never have to worry about dragging yourself out of bed in the morning again. You will leap from under the covers each morning! You'll feel the joy and exhilaration of discovering what the day will bring. This new idea will fill you with energy and ambition much like the excitement one feels in starting a grand new adventure—only you feel it every day!

Purpose is the why—why you do what you're doing. It is the basic motivator for your life. As you set about discovering what your purpose is, it is important to understand that it does not come from outside. You'll only find it in you. It is an innate part of your being. It can only come from within. You can't ask others what your purpose might be. All they can offer is their view of you based on their own beliefs. Just as you can never imitate someone else's passion, someone else cannot guess your passion. Some of them may even discourage you from chasing that dream because of their own fears or assumptions. As you look within at your talents and gifts, you must set aside any negative thoughts or 'practical' rationales. These are just fear in disguise. You cannot allow them to mold your future.

This type of searching has turned lawyers into authors and motivational speakers and computer programmers into high school teachers. There are literally millions of people just like you who may be frustrated and bored with their profession but feel stuck. They feel like one spoke on an ever-turning wheel doing their duty while sacrificing their own dreams and wants.

When you create multiple sources of income from a variety of sources, it gives you the freedom to fulfill those wants and desires without sacrificing your standard of living or shirking your responsibilities. It is all about choice. Once you find your purpose, you will find a way to fulfill it. You can't let fear convince you otherwise.

But what if you've tried before and failed? Every single person that you see or encounter has failed. This includes you, me, or any other successful person. It is important to understand that when we fail, it's not that our intentions are at fault—it's that our guidance system was off. We are not in harmony with what we were trying so it just didn't work. In this situation it's very tempting to think back to things we might have done differently. This is like running the 'what ifs' in reverse. What if I'd said this, or done that? This replay of the past is a complete waste of time. The past cannot be changed. But if you constantly live in a mindset of shoulda, coulda, woulda, then it will adversely affect your future.

Let's go back to the example of being stranded on the island with a dinghy. Let's say that you finally got up your courage and climbed in that little boat and pushed away from shore. You rowed and rowed as hard as you could but the current kept bringing you back to the island. Does this mean that land doesn't exist or that you were wrong to try? No! You did the right thing. You just went the wrong direction. Now, when you think of trying to get in that boat and start again, it's harder than it was the first time. There are even more doubts and fears to overcome—after all, you've already failed once.

If you've tried to create wealth before though a particular business or type of investment and it turned out poorly, you must not let your mind convince you that all business is bad or that it's not for you. You have to realize that you have the opportunity to try again and this time you will have your purpose to guide and direct you. Don't let others or your own past experience convince you to be satisfied with a life that is less than you want or deserve.

This will require quite a bit of creativity on your part. Many people find this part difficult. Most of us rarely exercise our creative thought process. This shouldn't surprise you. We're taught from our earliest days in school to conform rather than to be creative. We have to raise our hand in order to speak, color inside the lines and walk in line. We are taught to search for the 'right' answer rather than offer creative solutions. We take orders and do what we're told or suffer the consequences. This doesn't mean that school is bad. After all, the teachers must maintain some sort of order. But it does point out how this habit of doing what everyone else is doing becomes planted in our mind.

This means that you, as well as most of the people you know, will habitually do what is expected to maintain the status quo. It takes real effort to change or break free from this life—even if you are miserable. This training plants the seed for the *Attitude of Average* that most people carry with them throughout their lives. They aren't wonderful and they aren't awful—they are in the vast grey area in the middle.

I spent decades of my life thinking I wasn't very special. Nothing around me seemed much different from what others had and people repeatedly told me that I should accept my limitations and conform to what everyone else was doing. It was years before I realized that I had something that no-one else had. I had special talents and unique ways of looking at the world that were mine alone.

So do you. As you focus on your unique gifts, you will come to realize how complex and spectacular you are. Add to that the ability to mold a sculpture, program a computer, grow healthy plants, sing beautiful songs, calculate columns of numbers, speak in front of groups, choose stylish clothes and accessories, fashion furniture and cabinets from wood or write an emotional novel. All of your specific and unique gifts come together to create a one of a kind masterpiece called *You*.

Protecting the Seed

When you do find your purpose, and you will, it is important to understand that it is not time to get input from others. Your purpose is just the direction, and it is still a small seed that can be destroyed by others' opinions of what you should do with it. This happened to me years ago when I first decided to take what

I'd learned and share it with others. I'd been working at Nightingale Conant for about five years when the idea came to me that I wanted to do exactly what my close friend and mentor, Earl Nightingale, was doing. But I wanted to do it under my own name using the education and knowledge I'd acquired over all the years. So, I got a tape recorder and recorded my own thoughts on the subject of personal growth.

I was excited! I realized I had found my purpose. This concept energized my whole being. In my excitement, I went looking for feedback. I wanted someone to agree that this was my purpose and an absolutely fabulous idea. So I called up a good friend and told him I had a great idea I wanted to share. I took the tape and recorder up to his house and turned it on for him. He listened. He didn't say anything or offer any encouragement—he just listened. As the tape played on, the pressure in the room became enormous —it was his embarrassment for me. Eventually, I turned the tape recorder off. "Well, it was just an idea," I mumbled,

I can't tell you how depressed I felt. As I left his house, doubts and fears whirled through my mind that hadn't been there earlier. The 'what ifs' crowded in. What if I'm just kidding myself? What if I don't really have what it takes? What if I try it and my audiences react exactly as he did? As I was driving home, it finally hit me—I was letting him steal my dream! This was *my* dream! I was excited and exhilarated by this idea. I knew this was what my purpose was and that's when it clicked in my mind—I can do this. It doesn't matter what anyone else thinks or what their opinion is— this is mine!

Had I let that one encounter affect me, I might have disregarded my life's purpose as an unrealistic pipe dream. I would have kept building long-term visions in my head but I would have been going in the absolute wrong direction—and on some level I would have felt that. Even if I had set the idea aside, I believe I eventually would have become so unhappy that I would have revisited the concept and found the right path—my path. But it sends a chill up my spine to think how close I came to missing all that life had in store for me. I see people toss their dreams aside every day because of a negative reaction or comment from a friend or relative.

If you are not on purpose, everything is off course. You are rowing your dinghy into the middle of the ocean with no idea where land is. Once you have the right purpose, you'll easily develop the right vision and then recognize the specific goals that will get you what you desire.

Carol and Dan Gates are business partners of mine in Bob Proctor Coaching (www.BobProctorMoney.com/BPC). For years we have been helping people all over the world understand this subject, helping them discover their purpose and add real meaning to every area of their lives. If you're having difficulty discovering your purpose, don't be shy. Ask for help and we're more than willing to help you.

Once you've found your purpose, how do you express it? By creating and maintaining a vision. Vision is what you do with your life. Vision is the strategy behind the fulfillment of your purpose. You accomplish this strategy by creating several short-term goals to keep you on course. You can think about this process just like climbing a mountain. Your purpose is to reach the top of the mountain. Vision is much like a plan or map. It is the direction you will travel and the terrain you will navigate on your journey. Goals are the individual steps that get you there. You set goals that will get you to the next level. Then you stop and take a look at your map again.

Your purpose is still to get to the top of that mountain; the map shows that you are traveling in the right direction. So you set several more goals that will help you climb even higher. This allows you to accomplish great things. It also keeps you from wandering around trying different things that are unrelated to what you are trying to achieve. If, at any point, you aren't moving forward, it also allows you to step back and refocus on your purpose and see if you have gotten off course. That way, you can quickly correct the situation.

Don't think that every single step has to be clear before you begin—it won't be. Often, you will find that striving toward your purpose is much like driving in a thick fog—you can't see more than three feet in front of you. But as long as you know where you are going, you can make the entire journey this way, one step at a time.

I've had people stop me at this point and say that they have tried. They did everything that I suggested, but they are no closer to what they want. They defined their purpose and envisioned their new life. They did everything they could to create a wealthy mindset but nothing happened. They became exhausted from trying and eventually gave up. So what's the problem?

Usually, they're trying to ascend the summit when they haven't even made it to base camp. They are focusing on what they want and visualizing but they aren't actually doing the things that will get them there. They aren't plotting the little goals and steps necessary for them to climb the mountain. They haven't created a vision or a plan to even know what those goals should be. They probably haven't even bought any climbing equipment or sleeping bags! They just want the prize. They want to instantly be on top of the mountain without having to take the necessary steps to get there.

By now, you have to know that won't work. You must be willing to climb the slope to get to the peak. There are no shortcuts. Even if you develop a plan, you can't just set it aside and assume it will happen if you don't put any effort into it. You must be personally involved with making it happen on a daily basis. I frequently talk to people who are frustrated because their plan is plodding along so slowly. So I ask them to give me a listing of the number of hours they spent that week that were directly related to their goals. Some will say one hour, or five or even ten. There are 168 hours in every week. If you subtract out 8 hours per day for sleep that leaves 112 hours that you are awake and able to function. If, out of that time you are spending less than ten or even twenty percent working on your goals, it's no wonder that your progress is moving at a snail's pace! If you are not giving your dream the time it needs to fit into your life, then the dream will never *become* your life. You must reexamine your priorities and carve out more time for what is important to you.

Another common mistake is that people get so completely carried away with the details of plotting the goals and steps within their vision that they never progress beyond the planning stage. You will see this frequently. They talk about their plan and it sounds great, but they never put it into action because they are always trying to work out one more detail, one more unknown. This is often referred to as *Analysis Paralysis*. They get so caught up in planning, charting and graphing their future that they never actually **do** anything. This is nothing more than a way to hide from their fear. Your plan doesn't have to be perfect. Get the basic ideas in place and get moving.

Finally, I'll caution you to not lose sight of the fact that you're beginning an incredible journey. It is not just about reaching the top of the peak. It's about enjoying the climb. Remember that I said that wealth is not a destination of accumulation but a journey of growth and circulation. You will meet wonderful people who will add untold joy to your life as you travel your unique path. Take the time to cultivate those friendships and relationships that add to your quality of life.

Vision Can Take Many Routes

Don't confuse your purpose with your vision. If we go back to the example of climbing the mountain, your purpose is to reach the peak. It doesn't change in any way. However, there may be many ways to climb that mountain other than the one you're on right now.

People will often say that they thought they had honed in on their purpose, but, for some reason, nothing fell into place or moved them along the path. They mistakenly conclude that it's the purpose that is wrong, not the route they choose. Most of the time, the purpose is fine—it's the vision that needs work.

A quick reevaluation will tell you if it is the vision or the purpose that needs to be revised. Ask yourself the following questions:

- Have you followed your heart and been true to yourself?
- Have you refused to allow negativity or the opinions of others to sway you?
- Have you confirmed that these unique talents excite and energize you?

If your answers are all yes, then you have found your purpose. Now you know that it must be your vision that needs attention, and you must work to find another path to fulfill your dream.

I had a friend who illustrates this problem very well. My friend flew into Ft. Lauderdale, Florida, and rented a car to drive up to West Palm for a conference we were having. This friend had printed a map from the internet showing the driving route and set off with great confidence. He got on the interstate and called to say he was on the way and would be arriving in 20 minutes or so. We waited....and waited. And waited.

He glanced at his map and saw that he was to exit on Atlantic. He took that exit and drove to the beach; no hotel in sight. He drove up and down the street but still couldn't find it. Of course, anyone who has been to this part of Florida is aware that almost every town along the coast has a street called Atlantic—Atlantic Ave., Atlantic Blvd., Atlantic St., you name it—but my friend didn't know this and just took the first Atlantic that he came to.

He finally ended up on Highway 1 that runs along the coast and made his way to the hotel—an hour later. The point is that his destination didn't change. The route he took and the length of time he spent getting there did, but he arrived just the same.

If your current plan isn't working, you must exhibit the same determination to arrive at your destination or purpose. Can you imagine my friend calling to say, "Well, Bob, I drove to the beach and the hotel wasn't there so I went home." Of course not. Then why are you so willing to give up on your dreams the second you think you might have taken a wrong turn?

This is why it is important that you take note of the directional indicators that are trying to alert you to the fact that you're going in the wrong direction. They may not be as obvious as a vanishing hotel but they're still there. When you are not on the correct path to your purpose, or when your vision is unclear, you will feel badly about yourself and what you're doing. This is a clear indication that you're no longer making progress toward your purpose. Your intuitive mind is screaming at you and telling you that something isn't right.

There's a difference between encountering solid barriers and resistance as you pursue your dreams. When resistance arises, your old beliefs may temporarily come back to life to assure you that you're on the wrong path. They will argue that it wouldn't be this difficult if you were on the right path. They will then prattle on incessantly that they told you so and if you'd listened to them in the first place you wouldn't be in this quandary. While resistance is irksome, it is not negative, and you will feel that within your soul. This is your intuition telling you the difference. If you were on the wrong path, your intuition would allow negative emotions and feelings to arise as an indication that you have taken a misstep or wrong turn.

When you are on purpose, your vision guides you toward the good you desire and, through the *Laws of Vibration* and *Attraction*, the good you desire moves in your direction as well. As long as you feel good about what you are doing, you should continue to push through resistance to reach your goals.

The Lies We Tell Ourselves

More often than not, people have difficulty getting focused on what their true purpose is because they're already doing something exhausting day in and day out. It's not their purpose, but it eats up all their time and because of that, they're convinced they're on the right track because the bills are paid. Think again. Just because you have a 9-to-5 obligation and your bills are getting paid doesn't mean that you've figured out your true purpose. This fact, however, can often block or impede your progress toward that better and higher use of your time and talents.

As I've said before, some people feel stuck in their present circumstances and are afraid or reluctant to make a move because they just can't see how their purpose will provide for them and their family. When you add in the fact that we've all been programmed from the time we were children to believe it's better to be safe than sorry, then it becomes very difficult indeed.

When you think about creating wealth, it's not better to be safe than sorry. When you picture yourself reaching the end of your life, do you think you'll be happy because you had a safe trip or will you regret all the things you never did because you were afraid to try? Since you never stepped into the dinghy, you end up wondering what would have happened if you had taken the chance and molded your own future.

You may be thinking, "Well that's great for everyone else, but my ship is here. I can ride it to safety and never wonder how I'm going to get to land. Why would I take the risk of getting in that little boat just to find out if there might be something better?"

You may have a really wonderful job that earns you large

amounts of money. However, any time that you work for someone else and trade your time for money, you always run the risk of becoming expendable. We hear of companies folding and laying off employees every day. These employees have often invested their whole lives to get nothing but a severance package in the end. Just because your paycheck comes from someone else's bank account, that's no guarantee that it'll be there a year from now, or next month—or even tomorrow. We've been conditioned to view corporate jobs as secure—when they are anything but.

A New York Times poll found that 34% of households had experienced at least one layoff since 1980. It also noted that of the ones who had not experienced a layoff themselves, almost 60% knew a friend or family member who had been laid off. What does this tell you about job security in the corporate realm? There is none and never has been.

Yet owning your own business or getting away from the corporate environment is frightening to so many. I think it's much like the fear of flying. The fear of taking personal responsibility for creating wealth in your life is so scary that people create an irrational and untrue view of entrepreneurship. Wealthy people know this to be a big lie. They know you are at more risk financially by depending on someone else than you ever will be by becoming independent and self-supporting.

This does not mean that you should throw caution to the wind and jump off a cliff into nothing. I've seen people come to the realization of their true purpose and stop everything they're doing, quit their job and start on the path to a new life. While I admire their spirit, this is not something I recommend.

You can't pursue your purpose and focus on what you want if your basic needs of life are not met. Over the years I've seen a number of people quit their full-time jobs because they want to devote more time and energy to building up their plan. Within weeks, when they begin to see that their basic needs are not being met, they immediately worry about "making ends meet." Remember the *Law of Attraction*: This worry attracts disaster.

When your needs are met, you have the freedom to take action where and when appropriate. You don't feel forced or desperate. When you're enjoying this freedom, you're also free of the worry and fear that will rob your creativity. You don't lie awake at night planning your escape from your terrible life because you know it'll happen when the time is right. It's a lot easier to go to work at your day job when you know that it is just temporary and necessary to meet your needs while you swing your full plan into action.

Running the Numbers

Once you think the time might be right, it is absolutely essential that you sit down and decide what your true needs are before you take any drastic action. What do you need to survive—to pay for housing, to buy food, to keep the electricity flowing and the water running? I'm talking about just the essentials here—not the vacation you would like or the new spring wardrobe that would be nice. Just the basics—food, water, shelter—make a list and come up with a figure.

When you have that amount, set it aside for a few hours or a day and then come back and evaluate it again. Is there anything else you can cut? Do you really need satellite TV? Can you get a cheaper cell phone plan? Would it be less expensive to buy a treadmill to have at home rather than pay for a gym membership? Only you know what you need and what you can give up, either temporarily or permanently. I've found that when people first list what they need, a few of their wants sneak their way into the mix. So keep looking for things that aren't adding real value to your life.

Now it's time to play with that number, and see how to continue to meet your basic needs creatively. Remember the goal we discussed—making $1 million and learning how to work the numbers into a small and achievable amount. We're going to do the same thing here, but the numbers will be significantly smaller. Let's say that the amount that you come up with is $4,000 per month. Your number might be even lower, especially if you're single. If you divide that by 4.3 for a weekly amount, the number drops to $930—that's less than $133 per day. Now that you know what your weekly and daily minimums are, you can set about making a list of ways to generate the amount you need while freeing up more time to spend on wealth creation.

I know what you're thinking—"But **HOW**??" All of the reasons and excuses your old beliefs can come up with are probably bombarding your mind right this minute. Don't worry. That's normal. But let's just set those aside for right now and use a real-life example.

I know a couple, we'll call them Mike and Tammy, who both wanted to get away from their jobs and do what they loved. They wanted to run a camp for children with cancer. Mike is in construction and Tammy is a nurse. They sat and calculated their expenses and determined what could be cut. With four small children their budget was already stretched to the max. They went over and over their list, but found only 10–15% of the expenses could be cut—which was disappointing, to say the least.

They saw no way either of them could quit their jobs and still make ends meet. This isn't uncommon. It may even be your situation right now. Many people expand their lifestyle to meet their income level. This is why you may feel trapped. You don't see how you will ever quit because you think you need every single dime just to keep things going. But there is a way.

Mike and Tammy decided to see how they could free up more time. Tammy, as a nurse, found that instead of working Monday through Friday from 8-5 at the hospital, she could work three twelve hour shifts from Friday through Sunday. She could make almost the same amount, because weekend pay was higher than for weekday shifts. This meant she would free up four days each week to work on their plan.

Mike was a construction foreman so he worked long hours and found it more difficult to rearrange his time. However, after doing some calculations, he realized that he could take a relatively small pay cut and go back to work as a regular construction worker and work fewer hours with no weekends. He convinced his boss to let him work four ten-hour shifts Monday through Thursday; this let him be home with the kids the days Tammy was at work. This actually had a dual benefit. Since two of their children were in daycare it allowed them to cut that expense completely and lower the amount they needed each month even more.

I want to talk about Mike's choice for just a moment. There are people who would not even consider taking a step back from their current position. Why? Because of those old beliefs. They tell you your plan is completely backward, that you worked hard to get to this point. But if your hard work hasn't produced the life you want, then what good is a title or corner office? Don't allow the false allure of power or your own sense of pride to confuse you into staying in a position that isn't moving you toward your goal. Often taking a step back in pay or position will give you the time to go after your dream—and isn't that worth it?

Mike and Tammy worked very hard at their jobs and used their free time to find ways to generate passive income to cover their necessities. Mike loved construction so he used his knowledge to find homes that were in foreclosure. He fixed them up to rent. Since he could do the work himself it cost him very little, and each home that he rented produced income to offset their expenses.

Tammy slowly cut back her hours as more cash flowed their way from Mike's activities. She used her time to write a book about how to create a better quality of life for children with cancer. As a nurse, she had worked with these patients for years, and had unique insights and tips for parents. She printed the book herself, and convinced several local hospitals and pediatric specialists to purchase them to give to patients. This suited her talents and also furthered their purpose of creating a camp for these children to go to each summer.

Within a very short period of time Mike and Tammy's needs were being met completely through the additional income they had generated. They were both able to quit their jobs and start their camp for children with cancer.

This is just one example, but it illustrates that if you are willing to really pursue your purpose with passion, and do what others are not willing to, it **will** happen. There are many opportunities and you must be open to all ideas and willing to work for what you want.

The Bottom Line

What are you willing to sacrifice or endure in order to live your dream? The fact is, no matter how easily your purpose comes to you, you will have to make sacrifices in order to achieve it. If you never make your dream a priority or carve out any time to devote to it, it just won't happen. There's a common misconception that the word "sacrifice" is bad—that it means you're losing something. You're not losing here. When you choose to sacrifice something in order to move your life to a higher level, you just give up something of a lower nature to allow room for something of a higher nature. You can never climb the mountain if you don't step away from base camp, can you?

What would you sacrifice to obtain your dream, to be able to do what you love every day? I suggest sacrificing those things that are not vital to your survival first. These things—like satellite TV—fall away in the first couple of tries. Then I encourage people to start cutting things that aren't needed to achieve their purpose—time wasters like clubs you belong to. It won't kill you, or those around you, to say no once in a while.

You might give up something you enjoy, a pastime or hobby, in order to devote more time to creating your wealthy life. You might be willing to endure a temporary cash crunch in order to get things rolling. You might be willing to give up one or two nights a week in order to receive the education, training or certification you need to get you one step closer to your goal.

Ambition is the expression of your desire—it's the fuel that gets you from point A to point B. Unfortunately, some people see ambition as a dirty word and equate it with greed. This is entirely incorrect. You're not competing with anyone else—there is an infinite supply for us all! If you use your wealth and money to create more, then you are circulating—not stagnating—and the result is that more will come to you.

The only struggle is with your own limiting beliefs. You must be ready to battle them for your dream. You must focus and expect great results. Desire without expectation is nothing but wishful thinking. As long as your belief is steady and you focus on your purpose, you'll be able to create a vision and goals to get you there.

Chapter 4 REVIEW

- Purpose is the Why.
- Vision is the strategy.
- Goals are the specific steps that get you there.
- Your purpose is your internal guidance system.
- You must not fear change.
- Don't live in the past or allow others to destroy your dreams.

- You must be personally involved with your dream on a daily basis.
- If you don't make your dream a priority, it will never become your life.
- For assistance in discovering your purpose, visit www.BobProctorMoney.com/BPC

Chapter 5

The Great Illusion of Time Management

Much time and attention is given to the idea of time management these days. Everyone wants to know how they can fit more into their already-packed schedules. But there is no such thing as time management: Time is a static force that never changes. You can never make more of it. Really, the only thing you can do is to prioritize your activities to accomplish the things that really matter most.

You might think that this is merely a difference in semantics but it's an important distinction. Time management is about arranging what you do to fit as neatly as possible into the time you have available. Prioritizing is about focusing only on the tasks that really matter and cutting the rest down—or eliminating them altogether.

Another word often used is budgeting. Many of us use budgets to rearrange what we're already doing with our finances, rather than prioritizing what is important and eliminating what isn't. The exercise I gave you earlier about cutting down your expenses is a good example. You'll notice, in that entire chapter, I didn't use the word 'budget' once. This is because we were prioritizing what you must do in order to reach your goal. Budgeting is simply rearranging. I think that people use terms like 'time management' and 'budgeting' to convince themselves that they're accomplishing something, when really, they're just shuffling around the same old jazz!

Prioritizing involves making choices and decisions about every activity in which you engage to see if it adds value to your life or not. Let's try a little experiment. Look at your life right now and think of the activities that you are currently involved in and about what you want to accomplish with your life. I'm sure that you can probably carve out an hour or two here and there each week to work toward your goals. It may not be much, but it's something.

Now imagine that you went to the doctor and he told you that you had exactly one year to live. How does that change your priorities? Would you piddle around trying to accomplish your dreams in only a few hours per week? Would you work extra hours to try and get a promotion at work that would never benefit you? Would you save for a retirement that wasn't going to happen? Would you plan to take a vacation for two weeks next June and hope you made it? Would you sit in front of the TV tonight?

When you think your time is unlimited, it's easy to waste it. However, when that perception is altered and artificially shortened, time becomes very precious indeed. My point is that time is *always* precious. Whether you live to be forty or up into your nineties, there is still only a limited amount—and it will never seem like enough. This is why prioritizing is so crucial. You don't want your life to rush past in a blur of busyness that never accomplishes anything.

In order to begin the process of prioritizing, you must learn to look at every activity in your life in relation to time. Often people don't even think about money in relation to time, but they are intimately interconnected.

Many of us are enamored with the concept of a 'deal.' We want to get the best price for anything and everything. We convince ourselves that we must do so in order to make our money stretch as far as possible. What we don't realize is what this mindset costs in relation to the time it takes. For example, have you ever driven across town to save an extra ten cents on gas? Phoned the bank and waited on hold for over 10 minutes to protest a $2 fee you don't recognize? Searched online for hours for the best price for a flight? You might argue that these activities are what any responsible person would do; but let's look at them in relation to time.

Your vehicle holds 20 gallons of gas, and you drive across town to save $.10 per gallon. This takes you thirty minutes. You saved $2.00. Now if someone were to call you and offer to pay you $4 per hour for your time you would be insulted. But that's what you just demonstrated your time to be worth.

If you call the bank to save $2 and wait 10 minutes, then you are worth $12 per hour. If you search three hours online to save $30 on airfare, then you are worth $10 per hour. But wait, there's more to it than that. Not only are you devaluing your time to a ridiculously small amount, you are also experiencing what is known as "opportunity cost." This cost is the price you pay in lost time for being unable to fully implement ideas that earn passive income—or to put off implementing them because you think you don't have "time."

For example, let's assume you have a great idea for a website that produces income by providing readers timely newsletters and articles on parenting. You want to get the idea up and running, but you don't think you have 'time' because you're too busy. So you wait. A year goes by, then two. Finally you get things underway, and the website grows over the next year to produce $5000 per month in subscription and advertising revenue.

It's easy to look back and see what all those busy activities actually cost. Things like hanging out with coworkers, chatting on the phone, watching television, texting your friends, surfing the internet, and volunteering for committees. You felt busy—too busy in fact to insert a new business into your life—but what did all that busyness get you in relation to what it cost by delaying this idea? When you increase effectiveness and delegate or eliminate the wasted busyness, you increase your cash flow and have something to show for your efforts.

All these activities that 'save money' are really highlighting a mindset of lack and limitation. By focusing on the miniscule savings they produce you are missing the abundance that could be yours by concentrating on producing income. Remember, money is like flowing water. Why rush into the middle of the stream, just to grab a thimbleful?

Another great time waster: the old 'what if' game. You worry about the mights and maybes. You rerun past events through your mind repeatedly, wasting the present. There's a Mark Twain quote that I like: "I am an old man and have known a great many troubles but most of them never happened." The same is true for you if you engage in a great deal of emotional drama about things that are unknown or have already happened. You create troubles in your mind that have nothing to do with reality and waste precious time.

Time Consuming vs. What's Important

It is easy to assume that if a task takes a great deal of time that it is important. One of my favorite examples of this is email. How much time do you spend sorting, reading and answering email? If you are like me, you think of this as a virtual pit of time and energy. But many people are very attached to their electronic inbox. They spend hours composing email and constantly check for new messages.

If you were unable to check your email for seven days, would the world come to an end? NO. The same is true of voicemail. Think of when you were away or on vacation for a week and couldn't respond immediately. Did civilization come to a screeching halt? Did you really miss anything that was of vital importance? Probably not. Very few things are truly important or urgent, yet we get so wrapped up in the idea of instant communication. We perceive them to be of vital importance and they just aren't 99% of the time.

Technology has made our lives much easier in a number of ways. But the idea that anyone can contact you at any time, for anything, allows many people to waste your time with unimportant chatter. This is one of the reasons that the first person most business people hire is an assistant to deal with phone calls, email and correspondence. It is incredibly time-consuming and needs to be done, but is not near important enough to take you away from much more productive activities.

The best use of technology is in the automation of mundane tasks. This may show my age a bit, but I like to use the example of office automation. When I was a young man making my way in the world, offices had entire legions of secretaries—in fact, their need was so great that they had a battalion of young women on standby to fill in if someone was sick or missed a day. They called this a "Secretarial Pool." The need for this manpower existed because the everyday tasks associated with communication and running a business were so time-consuming and labor-intensive that just one secretary wouldn't do. There were no hand held tape recorders, so secretaries had to know shorthand in order to write down what you wanted to say and then type it up. They used typewriters that had no auto-correction or deletion possibilities. They made copies with sheets of carbon paper.

Just having a letter dictated, typed and revised could take hours. You know that with word processing as it exists today, it might take fifteen minutes. But the fact that it used to be much more time-consuming does not make it more valuable. I use this example to point out that though technology can create time wasters, it can also increase the quality and number of tasks you can accomplish. It is important to know the difference and recognize those technological advances that improve your productivity versus those that eat a large amount of time.

This brings up another subject that people frequently quiz me on. Do you need to learn the latest technology to have an edge in business? Yes and no. You don't need to learn the latest time management software to decide what is important and what is not. However, increasing your ability to use spreadsheets and programs effectively can help you stay organized and accomplish tasks more efficiently. My advice is that if certain technological advances move you closer to your goals, use them. However, if you use all the latest gadgets and flashy technology, yet don't actually **do** anything to move forward, then they are time wasters and nothing more. What you do is much more important than how it gets accomplished. Don't allow anything to get in the way of your forward progress.

The 80/20 Principle

Almost anyone with a management or economics background has heard of the Pareto Principle. This principle was first suggested by Joseph Juran, who was a leader in management theory. He suggested that 80% of your results come from just 20% of your efforts. This concept is very useful when evaluating your daily activities. One task that I've suggested for those trying to prioritize their life is to keep a log of every single activity that you engage in during the day and find the 20% that is producing the vast majority of your results. Once you identify these important tasks, then take a look at all the others. This is the list you need to reduce or eliminate. Most people find that there are at least 10% of their activities that are wasting enormous amounts of time. These should be completely eliminated. The remaining tasks should be consolidated and reduced to a specific time frame or delegated to someone else.

It's best to be extremely selective of where you put your energies and not allow yourself to be spread too thin. You'll be able to focus on the tasks that help you reach your goals quickly and not delay your success. While you may feel as if you lack time, you must take responsibility and know that it is really just a lack of priorities.

Once you make your list of activities, you may be surprised how much time you spend on things that are unnecessary or accomplish nothing. Don't be too hard on yourself. We are trained from childhood, now more so than ever, to fill every available minute with activity. We don't like being bored. Our mind needs stimulation. The problem arises when we aren't actively thinking about, or choosing, positive stimulation. We are, unfortunately, masters of inventing distraction.

Think about the environment that exists in the corporate world. There are a lot of demands that you have to meet whether you're interested in that activity or not—or produce anything of real value. You end up doing large amounts of "busy work" to justify your position. Have you ever been called to a meeting to discuss the best time to have a meeting? This type of ridiculous redundancy is a daily occurrence, as is the acceptance of a cubicle environment that does its best to dull the senses and remove any scrap of creativity.

There are constant studies released that reveal the amount of time wasted by employees surfing the internet or chatting by the water cooler. The bottom line is that a company can purchase your time, but they can't make you productive. After being immersed in this environment it is no wonder that people don't adequately understand the value of their time.

The ability to effectively prioritize the activities of each day means you have to value your time. It's a basic self-esteem issue. If you see your life as valuable and meaningful, then you will value your time as well. If you find yourself wasting a lot of time, you probably don't have a strong enough reason to manage your activities in the best possible way. If your life has no meaningful purpose or direction, then it's not likely that there will be a compelling reason to change. You might get motivated on occasion but your motivation to improve just won't last.

Time management programs can present an irresistible lure. They coax you with the promise of greater productivity, more free time, faster income generation and higher self-esteem. And indeed, some of those benefits may indeed be realized in the short term. But there's always the risk that you'll find you're investing more and more time in micromanagement activities like getting organized, creating objectives and learning the latest software. Actually *doing* the tasks that your program is designed to manage becomes almost an afterthought. Instead of helping you increase productivity, your new program becomes another aspect of "busywork"—a means to disguise low productivity.

This is a common problem for people who haven't yet identified a purpose for their lives—which is why I discussed finding a purpose first. A fancy program provides the illusion of productivity, but when you strip it down to its raw and unfiltered source, you find it's devoid of real purpose. There's nothing there. When you sum up all the tasks, they amount to nothing but busywork and trivial activities. Whether or not a person actually gets anything done is of little consequence in the grand scheme of life. They add to nothing and are completely forgettable. You must find your purpose first or any attempt to prioritize activities will be in vain—without purpose, you have no clear direction.

Once you understand your purpose, you can begin to create actions that align with it. But realize that prioritizing your activities requires you to decide what to do and then **do it**. Most tips and advice that you hear on time management focus on getting things done. But if you haven't decided on the best course of action, then engaging in a bunch of activities just makes you feel busy. It doesn't accomplish anything.

You may have experienced this frustration. You feel like you know your purpose but continually spin your wheels trying to accomplish it. This could be because of a disconnect between your conscious and unconscious mind. Your conscious mind feels your new ideas and purpose are correct, but your sub-conscious hasn't accepted it yet.

This happens frequently. Someone might come to one of my seminars and decide they want to change. But instead of working on changing their ingrained beliefs, they start with a whole slew of activity. They know something isn't working, but instead of resolving this conflict, they try to avoid thinking about it. They go through at least one—and sometimes many—unhealthy cycles of hiding the truth from themselves. They feel frustrated with their inability to move forward with a purpose that their sub-conscious doesn't fully agree with; and yet, they feel they have no choice but to follow it.

To illustrate this, let's use the example of having a job. We're taught from the cradle that we should grow up and get a job. You go to school, perhaps even college and then you get a job. You may know that this is not the path for you and that your path lies in entrepreneurship. But because of this belief, you set the idea aside and tune it out to follow the expected path. You go to work each day, but don't really like it. You'd rather not go to work if you could afford to do so. You dream of freedom.

When you look at the results that people who followed the accepted get-a-job approach have achieved, you will notice very few of them seem happy and fulfilled with their lives. At work, they may pretend everything is fine but privately they feel miserable and trapped. Every year it gets harder. Personally I don't think most jobs are very healthy, considering the fact that they tend to stifle and crush the human spirit. I'm sure there are exceptions, but those aren't the norm. Deep down it is as if each of us knows that we can achieve a better result including abundant income generation, fabulous career opportunities and a fulfilling family life, without the confines and demands of traditional employment.

The Method

Virtually every time management system teaches that you must prioritize your projects to make sure you're working on what's truly important; don't get caught up in minor things, it says. However, very few explain precisely *how*. How do you decide which task is really the most important at any given time? Is it the one that's most urgent, the one that will earn you the most money, the one that will produce the greatest long-term happiness, the one that will please your family the most? If you don't use an intelligent method of prioritization, you'll lack consistency and bounce from one task to another with no rhyme or reason.

The main objective is to make the greatest amount of progress toward your goals with the least amount of effort. There are many examples of methods you can use to achieve this and they all have a few things in common:

1. **Purpose**—In order to effectively prioritize, you must know your purpose or objective. If we go back and think about your purpose in relation to climbing a mountain, it is important to focus on getting to the top of the mountain. This does not mean you go around it or focus on camping at the base of the slope. You focus on reaching the peak and compare all your tasks to that one objective. The ones that move you the farthest and fastest toward that purpose go at the top of your list.

2. **Time**—As we've already discussed, time is your scarcest resource. You cannot ever create more of it. So when you evaluate your list, first consider the time it will take to complete each task in relation to the amount of forward progress that you will make. Those tasks that propel you forward in the least amount of time, with the greatest reward are ranked higher. It is also important to take into consideration if that time is flexible. Can you perform the task by utilizing short amounts of time that can be rearranged at will, or is it a set amount of time that must be performed in a set location?

3. **Other resources**—You should also evaluate the amount of other resources that a task takes to rank it even more specifically. These resources would include things such as money, family time, use of social network and physical energy.

For some, a grid with the tasks in a column on the left hand side, ranked in ascending order by time, can help. Put your resources in columns across the top. You can then rank each task against the resource with a numeric value, 1 to 5. The tasks that take the least amount of time and have the lowest score in relation to other resources are the ones you should focus on first.

For example, let's assume that you have released a great deal of weight recently and that you feel your purpose is to help others reduce their weight and live healthier lives. You might come up with some tasks like these:

1. **Develop** a website with articles about weight loss where users can chat, support each other, and sign up for my newsletter.
2. **Start** a blog about my personal experiences and struggles.
3. **Speak** to groups about weight loss.
4. **Create** a program for weight loss I can trademark as my own.
5. **Write** a book.

The first thing you would do is rank them according to the amount of time they take. So you might reorder the list to look something like this:

1. **Start** a blog about my personal experiences and struggles.
2. **Speak** to groups about weight loss.
3. **Develop** a website with articles about weight loss where users can chat, support each other, and sign up for my newsletter.
4. **Create** a program for weight loss that I can trademark as my own.
5. **Write** a book.

Your chart might look something like this:

	Money	Family Time	Social Network	Physical Energy	Total	New Rank
Blog	1	1	2	1	5	1
Speaking	1	4	2	4	11	5
Website	4	2	1	3	10	3
Program	2	2	1	3	8	2
Book	5	2	1	2	10	4

This exercise tells you that the first item on your particular list should be to start a blog. It takes very little time and no money. It takes nothing away from your family time, and very little physical energy. The only thing extra effort will be to send out email to your current group of contacts to let them know you have a blog, so they can start reading it and giving you feedback.

When you use those criteria, it's interesting to note that speaking moved from second to last. While you may be speaking at a function for only 30 minutes to an hour, it is more difficult to fit this into your life. It takes time away from your family, and it also takes a great deal of energy to prepare to talk in front of a group.

The website and book came in at the same ranking. In this case, to rank them, you would default back to the amount of time each one takes. When looking at the category of money, you have to overcome the urge to shuffle your tasks by which one is the cheapest. In this instance, it takes more money to produce a website or a book than to speak to groups. But you have to remember that you can always make more money—but you can never make more time. Therefore it is very important to sort by time first.

One frequent comment that many people make is to think that because it takes more TOTAL time to produce a book, then it should always outweigh the area of speaking. Remember when I said that time was not just a function of the amount of time that a project takes but also a function of flexibility? You can write a book using short 30-minute or one-hour time slots at any given point in a day. You can also rearrange those time slots if something else is more important on that day. Speaking must happen at a prescribed time and place, where and when that particular audience has agreed to meet. It has no such flexibility and can't be moved or arranged to fit your current schedule. This lack of flexibility is reflected in the chart by the amount of time it takes from your family, and the amount of physical energy you must expend.

Many people find the grid system a little overwhelming. You don't have to do something this detailed. You can simply create a list at the end of each day to accomplish the next day and keep these factors generally in mind. This allows you to focus on the absolutely essential tasks at the beginning of the day. If something doesn't get done, it will be those at the end of the list that aren't as critical. It doesn't have to be difficult or complicated. The important concept to understand is to have a clear way to rank what you do, and then set about accomplishing those tasks in their order of importance.

Decision Making

I've always thought it very sad indeed that our schools don't teach decision making as a skill. The ability to trust your instincts and make quick and accurate decisions is something that can be learned. The more you practice, the better you become at it. Decisions are all about choice and evaluation. We have many options as to how to complete our various tasks in life and we need to make choices. This is relatively simple and can be evaluated using the prioritization strategy we just talked about. We can determine the best option based on the given criteria.

But other decisions can be harder to evaluate. Sometimes we face tough choices that involve one or more unknowns. We can't know in advance what the consequences of each alternative will be. Often we can waste precious time trying to guess. This results in a great deal of lost time and, even worse, stagnation. This is especially true of what we perceive to be big decisions like quitting a job, starting a business or moving to a new city for better opportunities. But there is no way to know all the determining factors before leaping into the unknown.

Often, when presented with this, people experience an extended type of mental paralysis. The fear of the unknown leads them to put off any decision and procrastinate. Every decision involves a choice between maintaining the status quo—your existing beliefs—and making a change. Because we can't guarantee a particular change will work out for the better, by default, many of us stay put.

Once you are able to develop a wealthy mindset and set aside the chatter in the form of 'what ifs' from your existing beliefs, decisions should be quick—even big ones. Decisions are actually a direct reflection of who you are and what your purpose is. Each one confirms the beliefs you have about yourself and the direction you are traveling.

Sometimes we procrastinate on projects because we don't know where to begin. A goal like "write a book" might seem straightforward enough when first set, but when it's time to act, the goal becomes a huge pit of unknowns. Procrastination soon follows. One way to get beyond this is to focus on the step right in front of you. Once that step is complete you move on to the next step. For example, if you were writing a book about dieting, the first step would be to create a very simple outline that listed the content of each chapter. Once that is done, the next step would be to take the title of chapter 1 and list fifteen ideas that explain that chapter. The next step would be to list those ideas in logical order; then spend five minutes writing on each of the fifteen items.

By focusing on each step rather than the project as a whole, each portion comes together in a logical fashion and the overwhelming feelings associated with the idea of "writing a book" are removed! And in case you were wondering, this is exactly how the book you are reading right now was put together.

By breaking big concepts and decisions into little concepts and choices, it allows you to focus and make progress rather than procrastinate because it seems too big for you to accomplish. One solution that some people find effective is to break a large project down into a list of small steps, planning it all the way from beginning to end. These small steps are very basic action items— so small, in fact, that you'd be hard pressed to break them down any further without it being ridiculous.

An example of a small step is to make a 5-minute phone call concerning one aspect of the particular project, or to send an email to one of your contacts to answer a specific question. It is typically a task that can be completed in less than 30 minutes, and ideally in less than 10 minutes. Again, these are very small, well-defined actions.

You may be thinking that it isn't always possible to break a large project down into small steps before you start. But often, you don't have to reinvent the wheel. If you want to know how to write a book, you can find books with step-by-step instructions on how to do that. They don't break it down all the way to the level of these small steps, but they do come close and give you wonderful guidance to get started.

There are indeed situations where there's simply too much uncertainty to plan a project from beginning to end with any level of specificity. A good example is website development, which often works best with an interactive process. In such situations, you can still use small steps to plan out as far as you can reasonably see. Then when you reach a certain milestone, update your plan for the next stretch ahead.

When embarking on a big project, plan it out using small steps from start to finish. These lists can be several pages long and they may take some effort to create. Once the list is complete, though, it makes the implementation go much more smoothly. It also makes it possible to create accurate estimates of when a project will be complete. Remember how important it is to be able to see the finish line?

These lists can be really useful for projects that will follow a similar trajectory. If you're creating workout DVDs to complement your diet program, you'll probably make an entire series of them rather than just one. In this case, you would use the same process to finish every DVD in the series. By taking the extra time to create the list in the first place, you actually save more time in the long run. Making the next DVDs in the series will go very smoothly. You're able to focus on getting the project done without worrying that you might miss a vital step.

How do you decide when it's necessary to break a larger task down into many small steps? This decision should be based on the task's complexity. If the task seems clear, and it isn't so overwhelming as to create procrastination, then you can just put it on your daily to-do list and not break it down further. However, if it's new, unfamiliar or complicated, it may be in your best interest to break it down so you will have a clear idea of where to start. This will allow you to flow smoothly from action to action without having to stop and think about what to do next.

You may use some of these techniques or you may find ones that work better for you. It really doesn't matter as long as you have some way of prioritizing your tasks and evaluating your choices. After a while, you may become so accustomed to tackling large tasks that you can put something like "write a book" on your list without listing the steps. A proper plan with the right level of subdivision—depending on how far along the path you are—can be very motivating.

Action is Key

The first step in the whole process is to visualize your intention without having any idea as to how it will manifest. But once you do have a clear purpose, you must act. When those first few steps present themselves, it's your turn to cooperate with the manifestation process and prove to yourself that you're really serious. Otherwise, those action steps will just keep staring you in the face until you get off your behind and get to work.

When you create a task list for a project, you separate planning from doing. This helps the action phase go more smoothly, and it's easier to slide into a productive flow. You know that if you follow your plan, you're going to get a result. It may not be perfect but it will get done.

However, this is not an excuse for planning incessantly and never acting. The whole point of prioritizing and evaluating is to act—and act you must!

Chapter 5 REVIEW

- Time is your only nonrenewable resource.
- Focus on the tasks that matter and reduce or eliminate the rest.
- Prioritize by looking at each activity in relation to time.
- Increase effectiveness by decreasing wasted busyness.
- Use technology to improve productivity, not waste time.
- Lack of time is really lack of priorities.
- You must have a set system to prioritize tasks and evaluate choices.
- Action is key.

Chapter 6

Paradigms, Performance and Profit

Selfishness is not living as one wishes to live, it is asking others to live as one wishes to live. —Oscar Wilde

Many people often grapple with an elementary question: "If what people assume to be average results are so sub-par, why are they so popular?" By now, we know the answer: The majority of people have ingrained beliefs that are extremely hard to overcome. You'd think they would want nothing more than to break free from their mundane and mediocre existence, but they stroll through their lives accepting what is simply given. They refuse to believe there is more.

We've spent a great deal of time talking about conquering the old beliefs that are lodged in your mind. This work is internal, and must be done by you. However, be aware that, no matter what new ideas you incorporate into your life, you will be faced constantly with the paradigms of those around you and of society as a whole.

The word paradigm has been so overused, especially in the business world, that many people don't really understand its full meaning. A paradigm is a collection of beliefs that are held by a group of people. It's not just one belief held by one person. These beliefs are shared, passed on and believed by generations. Take the paradigm that you need to have a traditional job. Included in this paradigm are these ideas:

- You must have a job to be a contributing member of society.
- Those who put in many hours at a job are more committed and deserving.
- The better your education, the better your job.
- You must compete with your coworkers and be the best to move ahead.

These ideas are passed on in actions and statements by everyone around us. They're taught in our schools; most of us hand them down to our children. You may not think these ideas are central to your own life. But answer this: When you are first introduced to a new person how often do you ask where they work? If your child or relative says they have no interest in college, how likely are you to be concerned and ask them how they ever expect to get a good job? If someone tells you they are self-employed, do you wonder if they really mean unemployed and are less than motivated to work? All of these thoughts are evidence of how deeply rooted this paradigm may be.

Once you begin to question your assumptions and thoughts, you'll encounter something known as predictable divergence. At this point, you're able to see the truth—that these accepted paradigms aren't what you want for your life. And your change in mindset will separate you from those around you—those who haven't changed. This separation can be difficult. The unchanged around you will constantly try to bring you back to their way of thinking.

Fishermen will tell you that you can catch a bucket full of crabs and never worry about them escaping: Any crab who tries to climb out will be pulled back into the bucket by the others. This is how it feels when you try to strike out on a new path and in a direction of which others are wary. You may think they're doing all they can to get in your way and pull you back. But what they're really doing is projecting their own fears onto your situation. They may even feel that they are helping you—that they're steering you away from disappointment and failure.

If you want to accomplish what you want for your life, you must be able to resist this pressure. You have to do what others won't. You have to believe what they question and commit to stay the course. By moving out of the accepted norms and paradigms that society believes, you have an opportunity to investigate what life really has in store for you—not just accept the same old expected outcomes.

Crisis of Consensus

When you go against the expected path—the one others think you should follow—you can feel isolated. This is another widely-held paradigm at work, one I call the *Crisis of Consensus*. We are indoctrinated from our earliest years to believe that working as a team produces the best results.

To be fair, this can be true. If you have a sports team where the members are constantly pushing one another to greater heights, this works toward their collective good. They all have a common goal and an understood agreement as to how that goal will be accomplished. However, if you have a team where the path to the goal, or the goal itself, is undetermined, then something very different happens. As ideas are shared, the group will try to determine a path that all members of the group can agree on—not necessarily the one that will get them to a goal in the best or fastest way possible. The members who have very bold or avant-garde ideas will be brought down, while the members who have low expectations will be encouraged to participate and help.

As a result, the consensus becomes the action that will move them forward with the least amount of risk. Some of them may be sure what direction will be better, and others not. Since they can't agree, they come up with a solution that everyone can live with but no one is really happy with.

This is why I always say, if you're truly wanting to change your life, it's important to be around people with a similar mindset. If you constantly have to explain your actions and thoughts to someone who refuses to understand, your resolve will be worn down over time and doubts will constantly swirl around you.

While you have to be able to take criticism, it's more important to evaluate that criticism's source. If you're given caution or advised by someone that has experience in the area in which you're working, then you should listen and give their words significant weight. If the person has no experience, then you should let their words slide away and ignore them.

Performance and Profit

Almost every salesperson or business owner I know is interested in the connection between performance and profit. Nearly every system in the business world relates these two concepts in terms of cause and effect. If you do A, you will get B. So, it makes logical sense that if you want to achieve a particular goal, then you should create the actions that will produce that goal.

This is obvious and widely understood by most people—and completely wrong! When you are looking for a cause, it is almost never an activity—it's a decision or intention in the mind. For example, if your goal was to run a marathon, then you might assume that if you train very hard, your goal will be achieved. But if you really think about it, you'll discover that these actions also represent an effect. The real cause was the decision you made, and continually make every day, to run that marathon. Without this occurring first, you will never become involved in the training necessary to bring about the effect of running that marathon.

If you want to attain wealth, then you must first decide to do so. This is the first step in creating a wealthy mindset that will bring about your chosen result. The second step is to act. Missing this very simple distinction has contributed to quite a number of failed attempts. If you want to achieve a goal you've set, the most crucial part is to make the decision to bring it about and completely believe that it will happen. It doesn't matter if you feel it's outside your control. It doesn't matter if you can't yet see how you'll get from A to B. Those resources will show themselves after you've made the decision, not before. Always remember: Believing is Seeing, not the other way around.

If you don't embrace this concept, then you'll waste a lot of time. Step 1 is to decide not to play 'what if' or to ask around and see whether or not others think you can do it. If you want to start your own business, then decide to make it so. If you want to change careers, then decide to do it. If you want to add value to people's lives, then decide to do so. So many people waste so much time thinking that there has to be more to it. They often spend weeks, months or even years wondering if a particular goal is possible. But, if they had just decided and acted, they would have already achieved it. When you create this kind of doubt, you'll invoke the *Law of Attraction*. I guarantee it—but it will work against you.

Have you ever heard someone tell you one of their goals and you can just sense how uncertain they are? They say things like, "Well, I'm going to try this and see how it goes. Hopefully it'll work out okay." This is clear evidence that a decision hasn't been made. They are still in the pondering stage. If someone like this asked for your help, would you give it to them? Probably not—why would you waste your time on someone who isn't committed? However if that same person told you of their idea and you sensed that they believed in that idea and were totally committed to it, how eager would you be to help then? We often talk about the fact that enthusiasm is contagious and we all want to be around and help those who are committed to their goals and dreams. You're far more likely to do whatever they ask of you because you can tell they're eventually going to succeed anyway. You want to be part of that success! You feel energized and motivated to contribute to the success of people who are very clearly committed to a goal that resonates with you and which clearly adds value for others.

The connection is very clear between mindset, performance and profit. They are all interconnected and they do not exist by themselves. If you have a wealthy mindset but never act, then how will you achieve any sort of profit? If you run around trying to achieve your goals, but in your mind doubt that it can happen, you will fail. You will not have all the creative power your sub-conscious can unleash if you don't believe in what you are doing. When you've made a clear, committed decision, it will open the universal floodgates, bringing you all the resources you need, sometimes in seemingly mysterious or impossible ways. Whenever you want to set a new goal for yourself, start by making a decision to meet that goal and visualize yourself meeting it. Create the belief and then take action to make your dream happen.

Expectation will reward you but you must be clear on your intentions and committed to what you want. It's like planting a seed in the ground. You don't plant that seed and then say, "I wish that seed would grow." You simply plant the seed and expect that it will grow as a natural consequence of your planting and tending to it. Intend your goal. Manifest it in such a way that it adds value for all those who encounter you. This is very important. Goals that are created out of fear or a sense of lack will bring terrible consequences.

If you are trying to achieve goals but you're purely focused on the action steps without the correct mindset, then you're sabotaging yourself. If you go on a diet and exercise like crazy, while at the same time thinking, "I'm fat. It's hopeless. It's taking too long," then your thoughts will override your actions and negative or unremarkable results will follow. If you want to achieve a goal, you must clear out all the "hopefully" and "maybe" and "can't" from your mind. You cannot allow yourself a negative thought, which takes constant vigilance and practice.

Not believing in yourself simply means you're using your own power against you. It's like you're begging the universe to become wealthy by saying, "Let me be destitute," and you don't even realize it. If you think or intend weakness, you manifest weakness. If you project your power outside yourself and onto the external world by blaming others or external forces, you lose your power.

Commit to Action

Belief does not sit on the couch and wait for success to show up! You'll hear about people who focus so much on using the *Law of Attraction* through their mindset that they don't pay much attention to the idea of action. To talk about mindset alone only gives part of the story and it can lead some to believe that their responsibility is done. Success requires action and a strong work ethic—not a passive and irresponsible attitude.

The most common excuse among those with a passive attitude is lack of time and opportunity. We've already discussed the idea that lack of time is really a lack of priorities. As far as opportunity, well, more opportunities are available every day for people to develop their abilities and achieve success than ever before. The internet and the ability to start a home business for little to no money render this excuse worthless. Unfortunately the number of people who choose to make excuses rather than take action is tremendous.

When most people are not faced with a situation that is urgent or immediate, it's easy for their old belief systems to make excuses and convince them to never change. However, when faced with a potentially life-threatening set of circumstances, where we simply have to do something to survive, all excuses disappear and we become creative and successful in our problem-solving efforts.

A good example of this is a situation encountered by a woman named Nancy.

For years, my husband and I had seen the real estate guys on TV talk about how you can get into real estate investing with no money down. We even ordered the system they touted and agreed it was a good idea. At the time, my husband was in sales and I was an executive assistant. We thought that when the time was right, we'd do it. Then we set the idea aside. Life crowded in and we were both busy with our jobs and our children were young. We lived a nice life and didn't really want for much. We didn't have any real reason not to try it, but we also didn't have a compelling reason to do it either.

Then my husband had a heart attack, which was devastating. His heart was damaged and his recovery stretched out over many months. Since his sales were commission-based, we lost that income. We were forced to look for a way that we could create income that didn't involve him being physically active. The only thing we had in the house was the program we'd ordered on real estate. While I was at work he was able to learn more and then put it into action working the phone and having me do the legwork.

I was amazed at how quickly we accumulated properties while investing next to no money. In just a few months we were able to have a good income stream. By the end of the first year, we'd completely replaced his income, which allowed him to stay at home and manage our investments. It was much less stressful than his old sales job. At the end of the second year, I quit my job and we now live what I would call a very wealthy life.

We frequently discuss the fact that those DVDs had been on our shelf for almost two years and we ignored the opportunity until we felt forced. What were we thinking?

Nancy's experience isn't unusual. Many people investigate opportunities or businesses that could make them millions, yet they never pursue the ideas or put them into action. The problem is that they haven't made that solid commitment or decision to do so.

Taking Your Eye Off the Ball

The connection of mindset, performance and profit is clear when you look at salespeople. Over the years, I have worked with many salespeople, in the insurance industry in particular. Agents often blame outside circumstances for their failure to sell. It's always something: The location wasn't right, their prospect isn't interested. Some even cite their own lack of intelligence or money. On and on and on it goes. Those of you who are familiar with sales and marketing know exactly what I'm talking about. You can almost feel the different energy with each office based on the assumptions and attitudes of the sales people there.

An interesting anomaly, rarely noted, is that top performers are rarely present or participate in the general gripe sessions with their colleagues. In fact, they rarely associate with them at all. Top sales people have learned, often through trial and error, how important a positive state of mind is. They protect themselves from the negative energies given off by the rest of the staff and focus on their goals. This is frequently known as "keeping their eye on the ball." If they lose sight of their goal and immerse themselves in the excuses that other salespeople use, then their results suffer.

It's common for a salesperson to go through slumps and for their income to swing rather wildly. Many managers mistakenly try to correct this problem by arranging additional training so the salespeople will begin to perform again. If you understand the link between mindset and performance, you quickly realize that additional 'training' is useless. The salespeople haven't suddenly forgotten how to sell! They have lost the *belief and expectation* in their ability to sell. They've slid back into a negative mindset; they've focused on the lack of sales rather than focusing on meeting their goals. By worrying about what they don't want to happen, they've attracted that specific result.

Top performers understand the effect of allowing others to influence their mindset. By segregating themselves as much as possible, they protect their mindset and their performance not only remains high but is much more consistent without the wild swings in income. It makes no difference if you are a business owner, salesperson, consultant or anything else. What you believe will manifest in your life. If you lose sight of your purpose or allow outside influences to affect your mindset, it will affect your ability to perform.

Opportunities exist and always will exist. The question is whether you can see them and accept their challenge before they fade away. If you don't take advantage of the opportunity when it's offered to you, it passes you by like it never existed at all. Mark Twain said: "Those who buy books but don't read them have no advantage over those who don't know how to read." Like Nancy experienced, an opportunity placed on the shelf to gather dust doesn't help you. That said, understand too that just because you miss an opportunity does not mean that there will never be another. They are everywhere if you know how to look.

Experience

As you look at successful people, it can seem that they have a natural gift for wealth. It's easy to wonder if they are born with a certain innate knowledge or if this knowledge is acquired through experience. Do we have to experience many failures and mistakes before we can finally learn the skills necessary to really make it?

It's important to know that no one is given a free pass at birth. No one is born a top salesperson or brilliant business person. There is no such thing as a born winner, but there is also no such thing as a born loser. While it's true that everyone has certain hidden abilities, they must discover and develop them or they will remain forever dormant and useless.

Some people are gifted, more than others, in certain areas. You may even have a talent for *something* that you have yet to uncover or fully realize. However, it might surprise you to know that research has proven, in the vast majority of cases in which a person has created their own wealth, that only 10% of their success is talent and the remaining 90% is belief and hard work.

There are many who believe that Tiger Woods is a born golfer. And there's certainly no denying his talent. But he first appeared nationally on the Mike Douglas show in 1977 shortly after he started playing at age 2. He played for hours each and every day. He won his first major professional tournament in 1997. That's 20 years later.

If you started working toward your dream and spent hours on it every day, how would you view your success 20 years from now? How would you react when people called you a born winner? Since when does such predetermined success require twenty years of hard work? It doesn't. Tiger makes it look easy because he's had decades to perfect his game. He still practices every day and takes nothing for granted. It is a great example to follow. No matter how easy it looks for someone else, there is often much sweat and hard work behind what you see.

Tiger focused his interests and chose to do what he loved. He practiced and perfected his technique for years. His interests led him to discover a natural ability and he developed and cultivated his talent into success. A tremendous amount of effort (though doing what you love never feels like effort), will power, self confidence, time and repetition were necessary for Tiger to reach his present status of a "born golfer."

If the power of your interests and desires are strong enough, nothing you have to do to achieve your goal will feel difficult. Everyone can endeavor to be an expert in his or her field. Fortunately, not everyone has the same dreams, interests and goals. It is essential to do what you really want to in life, because desire is the catalyst that transforms work into pleasure. Having an above-average talent in any given area is only an advantage in the beginning, where growth comes faster with less effort. Once you reach a certain level, practice and the resulting experience become more valuable. You can substitute practice and endurance for talent, but talent alone can never replace hard work.

Never forget, those wealthy individuals that you look up to today have had their failures and setbacks—many have had more than most! Failures don't have to be negative. In fact, they're often the stepping stones to greatness. Only on the heels of such failures do they achieve such depth of success. Learning is the basis for good decisions; and we gain this knowledge and experience by making many mistakes. Good decisions are based on good judgment and experience. Experience comes from "exercising" bad judgment as well as good. Don't discount your unsuccessful attempts, for they will eventually bring you success.

A successful person who will always make the right decision has never existed nor will they ever exist. The successful person is unique in that they look at their failures with the awareness of a learning experience, allowing each one to hone their judgment and decision-making skills. Each failure brings them one step closer to the top. The unsuccessful person doesn't learn anything and never moves beyond their failure.

Successful people do not consider bad decisions to be a waste of time, money or energy, but rather an important learning experience. Rejection doesn't bother them much. They are even happy to receive a refusal, identify a misunderstanding or catch a mistake early in the game because it is easier to correct and they will spend less energy heading in the wrong direction. They redirect their energy into a positive direction and head toward new possibilities. If you adopt this mindset, no one will be able to stop you from becoming wealthy.

I can tell you that success is always sweeter when contrasted by our failures. A person that rises to wealth from nothing appreciates his new lifestyle in a way that someone born with money never can. Eastern religions say that there is no good without bad, no beauty without ugliness, no success without failure. It is these two extremes, opposite yet part of each other, that perfectly balance life and make it work. They call this the yin and yang. Without beginning, there is no end. There can be no beginning without an ending first. The end, as T.S. Eliot once wrote, "is where we start from."

Successful people embrace both extremes and know them as equal parts of the same whole. They learn their characteristics, raise their awareness and accept them as part of themselves. This is why they are able to see opportunity in the midst of failure.

They are not distinguished from the unsuccessful by experiencing fewer disappointments or fewer failures in life. They know opportunity is there and they merely set aside the negative emotions of failure in order to look for the good. Successful people use the same experiences as everyone else, only they view them through their wealthy mindset, and they become signs that guide them on their path to success. The non-wealthy mindset sees them as proof of their failure to achieve.

Big Dreams, Big Mistakes

Wealthy people own their own businesses. In order to have a basic understanding of how they became successful, you also have to have an understanding of some of the biggest mistakes they have made. I've built the following list from my own experience, as well as the experience of other wealthy people. As I coach people to start their own businesses, I often see many of them make the same mistakes. These tips are geared toward small business owners, particularly people who are just starting (or about to start) their own business.

1. We All Sell

Every person sells. It doesn't matter if you sell a product or not. A mother sells the idea that vegetables are great to their children. Politicians sell their idea of change to the voters. Charities sell the idea of their cause to donors. Sales simply involves bringing others around to your way of thinking. While sales are important to the survival of any business, you don't need to push your business on everyone you meet, including friends and family. Furthermore, it's a waste of time to try selling to people who simply don't need what you're offering.

One of the first mistakes some new business owners make is trying to sell to *everyone*. Some customers are much easier to sell to than others. For example, a friend of mine is a business consultant. He knows that if a potential customer is broke and obsessively worried about every nickel they spend, or if they are convinced that the problem is outside their company and resist the idea of changing their mindset, they won't be a good client in the long run. The 80/20 rule applies to customers the same as it does other areas of life: 20% of your clients will cause 80% of your problems. If you can weed out these problem clients up front, do it! Don't feel like you have to say yes to everyone you meet. By being selective, you'll save yourself many headaches and free up more time to focus on serving the best customers.

Early in my career, I probably said yes to the majority of the people who approached me with a potential business relationship. I wasted a great deal of time pursuing deals that were too much of a long shot. I accepted lunch invitations from various business people who just wanted to see if there was some business we could do together. Virtually none of them made me a dime. If you think a meeting is pointless, it probably is. Don't network with random people just because you think you're supposed to. Today, I accept such invitations much less often. If an offer doesn't excite me right away, I usually decline it. You must say no to the weak opportunities so you have the capacity to say yes to opportunities with greater promise.

2. Buying a Job

Some may think I talk about passive income way too much. But the truth is, to create real wealth, you must understand that cash flow is king. Many new business people start up or purchase a retail business that not only takes all their available cash, but also takes all of their time. In effect they have done nothing but buy themselves a new job. Since many traditional businesses take 3 to 5 years to start being profitable, owners spend a great deal of time working for free. Until you have steady cash flow coming in, don't spend your precious start-up cash unless it's absolutely necessary. There are many businesses, such as network marketing or affiliates, which require very little start up cash and provide quick returns and steady cash flow.

Your business should put cash into your pocket. Before you "invest" money in it, be clear on how you're going to pull that cash back out again. In the age of the internet business you can very easily start a lucrative business for pocket change. That cash flow can then support any other business ventures you might wish to undertake.

3. Being Too Cheap

Just because you can get things started relatively cheaply, that doesn't mean you should remain tight fisted. If you want your business to grow, there are things that are worth paying for. Don't let frugality get in the way of efficiency. Take advantage of skilled contractors who can do certain tasks more efficiently than you can. Buy good equipment when it's clear you'll get your money's worth. You don't have to go overboard with office furnishings, but get something functional that helps you be more productive. Don't use an old computer with outdated software that slows you down if you can afford something better.

It takes time to develop the wisdom to know when you're being too cheap or too free with your cash. If you're just starting out, ask someone with more experience. Often the very thought of getting a second opinion makes the correct choice clear in your mind. If you can't justify the expenditure to someone you respect, it's probably a mistake. On the other hand, there are situations where it's hard to justify not spending the cash.

4. The Real You

If you're new to business, don't pretend you're anything else. Don't fake your experience level. Some newly self-employed people think they must become actors and create an aura of experience that they don't really have. Trying to fool your clients in this way will come back to haunt you. People can sense when someone is less than honest and even those that believe you will find out the truth at some point. If you're so desperate for business that you need to lie, you shouldn't be starting your own business. If you can't provide real value and charge fairly for it, then you're not ready to open your business. Develop your skills a bit more first.

5. Forgetting the Relationship

Sometimes it is easy to forget that a contract is not a relationship. No matter how much legalese you put on paper, it comes down to a relationship between people. In the end, a contract is just paper and ink. It's common for contracts not to be honored. But it usually has to do with a breakdown of the relationship. I've known many business people who focus so much on trying to force clients to honor contracts that it destroys the relationship completely.

Often when a dispute arises, it can be worked out with a face to face meeting. News that a client isn't doing what they promised is your first signal that the relationship is in trouble. You should take the extra time required to correct the problem.

If the relationship is destroyed, the contract won't save you. The purpose of a contract is to clearly define everyone's roles and commitments. But it's the relationship, not the threat of legal action, that ultimately enforces those commitments.

The most creative and lucrative business deals almost always stray from the paper contracts that represent them. Business relationships are similar to other personal relationships—they are dynamic and change all the time. That's not to say that written contracts are unnecessary, but they're secondary to relationships. Just don't make the mistake of assuming that the contract is the deal. The real deal is the relationship. Keep your business relationships in good order and you won't have to worry so much about what's on paper.

6. Ignoring Your Gut

You might think that logic is the underlying driver of business. Not true. If you base all your business deals on hard logic and ignore your intuition, you will not become wealthy. You may do okay but you won't do great.

Humans never use as much logic as we like to think we do. We simply don't have enough data to make truly logical decisions. Why? Because business deals depend on human beings and we don't have a logical system for accurately predicting human behavior. Not being able to predict how other people will behave in a given situation removes logic as a tool. Intuition has to fill that gap.

It's hard to say no to a deal that seems lucrative by the numbers when my gut is warning me away from it. But I've discovered that often I see evidence later that my intuition was right all along. Intuition is a critical part of the decision-making process in business. Since business deals depend on relationships, you must learn to read the other people involved in any deal you consider. If you get a bad feeling from them, walk away. If you get a good feeling, proceed.

7. Tux vs. Business Suit

In some settings, a certain degree of formality in business is appropriate. But in most business situations, being too formal can get in the way. Business relationships work best when there's a good person-to-person connection.

I think it's a mistake to be too formal, even when looking to establish new business relationships. People don't want to build relationships with faceless corporations or entities—they only want relationships with other people. Treat your business relationships like friendships or potential friendships. Too much formality puts up walls, and walls must be torn down to create good business relationships. Formality can also be boring and tedious. You don't want your clients to merely endure your presence. If you demonstrate that you have a real personality and a good sense of humor, a connection is far more likely.

Many new business people take themselves much too seriously. They think acting "businesslike" means being stiff, formal and unnatural. Be careful. This can create an awkward and uncomfortable environment and that can make it hard for your customers to do business with you. Don't be afraid to show your personality. It can help people relax. Ultimately, you'll enjoy your work much more if you attract the kinds of clients that want to work with you for who you are. So, never be afraid to show your real self.

8. Create Value

Here's an easy trap to fall into: Thinking the purpose of a business is to make money. Think all the way back to the beginning: It's not about money. I've said that over and over again and in this context it's equally true. The real purpose of a business is to create value. In the short run, you might be able to make money without creating much value. But, in the long run, it's unsustainable.

Your business has to provide some sort of value, both to you and your clients. The better you understand the value you're trying to provide, the better you'll be able to define the clients you want. Too often business owners aren't clear on the value they're trying to provide—they just want to sell products. The world doesn't need more products—but it always needs and wants genuine value creation. And that's where you should direct your efforts.

Although value creation is essential to a sustainable business, it's not the only significant factor. You have to find a way to deliver your value cost-effectively. Most likely, your first attempt won't be exactly as you had hoped. You'll waste too much time, money and resources trying to produce and deliver your value. And that's okay—you're learning. A great many businesses start out just like that and then learn to be more proficient and efficient as they go along. You will, too. It takes significant effort to build a successful business, but it's also a tremendous growth experience. Sometimes you'll wish there were shortcuts, but the lessons learned and experience gained will push you that much further along the path to wealth.

Chapter 6 REVIEW

- You must do what others won't, believe what they question and commit to stay the course.
- Spend time around those with a similar mindset.
- In order to be wealthy you must first decide to be so.
- Create the belief and then take action to make it happen.
- There is no such thing as a born winner or born loser.
- Talent alone can never replace hard work.

Chapter 7

Freedom—Shatter the Pattern

We are creatures of habit. This can manifest in simple ways, as the type and number of restaurants we frequent or as complex as the companion we choose. We often make a decision to change our patterns, only to find ourselves sliding back into them shortly afterward. Real change requires strong and continued commitment.

There is an undisputed link between commitment and reward. Big goals demand big effort. If the effort is average then your reward will be, too. However, some find big goals intimidating for that very reason—they demand big effort.

The Comparison Paradox

As we discussed in the previous chapters, money is a commodity of exchange. It doesn't change—it only makes you more of what you already are. It will make a good person a great person and a bad person a terrible person. If you consider yourself to be a good person, then becoming rich will not only help you, but it will also allow you to help others. In order to make life better for those around you, you must seek wealth for yourself. You cannot give what you do not have. Unfortunately so many people are caught in their 'keep up with the Joneses" lifestyle that they sacrifice true wealth for what they can get right now.

It is natural for all of us to compare ourselves to those around us. Since most of us carry around an *Attitude of Average*, we view our lifestyle as being within a range of what's comfortable and comparable to our friends, neighbors, parents and siblings. But what it really means is that we're limiting ourselves through comparison to others.

We create within our own mind an idea of the "obtainable" rather than the "possible." So when we set goals, we start out by deciding what is obtainable and then take steps to achieve that limited goal. A good example would be if you look at your bank account and income statements of what you earned last year. That represents what you know you can earn. Then, you might decide to stretch a little to what you think you can earn and set your goal there.

This goal may only be 5-10 % higher than last year. The problem isn't that you can't meet that goal—you can! And maybe *that's the problem*—the goal is too limited to begin with. Instead of contemplating what you really want you force yourself into a series of very small steps to reach what you think you can achieve. Since these are small goals they require small effort and don't really move you forward.

The comparison paradox arises frequently in the business arena as well. Each year, executives in almost every company I know will try to make projections for the next year's sales. They'll set a goal 5-10% above the current year. This is extremely low but they're trying to set a goal that they know they can meet and with the least amount of effort. Often the board or company owners will ask for a much more aggressive goal of 30% or better and then 'settle' back to 20%. This becomes more a prognosis than a goal. Instead of striving to be number one in the market they only strive to improve upon last year's performance. The 20% becomes their best case scenario. What if they aimed for the top—even if it meant doubling their sales? This projection of 'achievable' limits what is possible prior to even trying.

The problem with the comparison paradox is that it allows us to believe that we are setting goals and making progress—which is a good thing in most people's minds. But in reality, it limits us to a predetermined outcome and cheats us of our true potential. It also sets up an endless pattern of settling. We achieve insignificant goals with little effort and when we achieve them, we set more insignificant goals as a follow-up. This is what makes us feel secure. But we end up stuck in this cyclical pattern, frustrated with our slow progress and at a loss as to how to fix the problem.

The irony of this situation is that, when challenged with a big goal, the response is one of disbelief. We're already so busy, how can we possibly achieve a goal that is many times higher than what we're already doing? People in these shoes need to prioritize and eliminate all the things in their lives that consume energy but produce next to nothing.

Any task that you have to accomplish will swell in perceived importance in relation to the time needed to accomplish it. This is known as *Parkinson's Law*. How many times have you been given a ridiculously short deadline for a project but you were still able to complete it—and complete it well? Short deadlines force us to focus and produce, which we could do much more frequently if we chose to. This allows for compression of projects into less time. But it does take focus.

This is where making a daily list of tasks can be a huge help. By checking off tasks as you finish them, you keep from becoming distracted and losing focus. This ability to self-motivate and keep yourself from falling back into the habit of wasting time is a cornerstone of self employment and true wealth.

Changing Your Patterns

There have been times in your life when you decided to make a change. Maybe it was to quit smoking. Maybe it was to go back to school. You know it's a change for the better, and you feel committed to it. Six weeks later, you realize that you have let the idea slip away and have fallen back into your old habits.

Because our paradigms and old beliefs are so ingrained, deciding we want to change often isn't enough. Even committing isn't enough. I ran across a study conducted by Brigham Young University in 1993. It compared the statements a person made about a particular change in their lives to the likelihood of them actually incorporating it. The results were as follows:

- Of those that made the statement "That's a good idea." They only had a 10% chance of making a change.
- Of those that committed and said, "I'll do it." They only had a 25% chance of making a change.
- Of those that said **when** they would do it, they had a 40% chance of making a change.
- Of those that set a **specific plan** of how to do it, they had a 50% chance of change.
- Of those that committed to **someone else** that they would do it, they had a 60% chance of change.
- Of those that set a specific time to **share their progress** with someone else, they had a 95% chance of change.

This illustrates how powerful it is to be accountable to someone. Accountability greatly increases your chances of doing what you say you are going to do. This is why it is so helpful to work with a coach or mentor. They'll hold you to your word and ask hard questions if you aren't measuring up to your own expectations.

We frequently let ourselves off the hook way too easily. We make excuses and create the logic that allows us to quit. While it may take some work to find a person that believes enough in your goals to hold you accountable, it's worth the effort. I frequently encourage individuals to seek out the support of a Mastermind Group. This is a group of individuals who have similar goals and aspirations. If you have regular meetings to share your progress and get support, it makes you accountable. And this can mean the difference between you succeeding or having setback after setback.

For many people, the idea of joining a Mastermind Group is a real departure. But often a departure is necessary to really move you forward. If you could become a millionaire all on your own, you'd already be one. Getting help can be the best avenue to learn quickly and have resources to draw on if you come up against something unexpected.

Step Away from the Resume!

Having a job is probably the most difficult paradigm of all for most people to overcome. It trips up more would-be millionaires than almost anything else. Even when they think they've changed and started a new business, they often find they have merely bought themselves a job. They still don't really understand the basic principles of passive income. Getting a job and trading your time for money may seem like a good idea. In fact, the vast majority of people will tell you that it is. However, when you start with the idea that time is your only non-renewable resource, then it seems awfully counterproductive to trade your most valuable commodity for a set amount of money.

If you have a job, you only get paid while you're working. That makes true wealth hard to generate. Passive revenue streams allow you to make money around the clock, leveraging your time to its fullest advantage. Just think how wonderful it would be to get paid while you were eating, sleeping or on vacation. If you plant a seed, doesn't it grow even if you're not there? Doesn't the river flow when you aren't looking? Money has the same ability.

This idea that we should work 40 hours per week is arbitrary. It's just fabricated nonsense. Who cares how many hours you work each week? If it took me one year to write this book, would you think it worth twice as much as if it took me six months? Of course not. If you provide something of value to people, they won't care how long you worked to produce it.

You'll want to build sources of revenue that generate passive income on a continual basis. There are many ways to do this. They can include starting a business, building a web site, becoming an investor, generating royalty income from creative work, network marketing or affiliate programs. These deliver ongoing value to people and generate income. The best part is that they are, for the most part, passive. Once in motion, they run continuously, whether you tend to them or not. Once you have one, or several, passive income streams, the bulk of your time can be invested in increasing your income by refining the existing income sources or creating new ones—instead of merely maintaining your income.

The internet provides many opportunities for passive income streams. It may take some time to get up and running, but a good value-based website can create thousands of dollars every month while providing readers with great information and tips. Registering a domain name is relatively inexpensive, and most of the tools necessary to run the site (blog, shopping cart, etc) cost next to nothing. While you may not earn thousands at first, everything beyond your start-up investment is pure profit so what do you have to lose?

It is important to recognize that you don't have to invent the light bulb to have something people will value. Look around and see what has already been successful. Go with a sure thing. Once you get it started, you won't have to work so many hours to support yourself. You'll be able to use that time to come up with even more ideas. Your local bookstore is filled with books containing workable systems that others have already designed, tested and proven effective. Nobody is born knowing how to start a business or generate investment income, but you can easily learn—and you are surrounded by the tools to do so.

It's important to remember that you don't have to hit the ball out of the park on the first swing. This isn't all or nothing. If your first attempt only generates a few hundred dollars a month, that's a significant step in the right direction. It doesn't mean that it is all you can do, or the best you can do—it's just the first step.

Because we're conditioned to think that a traditional job is the best way to make money, we often get hung up on the idea that we must have experience to be self employed. Completely untrue. You gain experience from living every day and learning lessons that can be applied to every area of life—including creating income.

The problem with getting experience from a job is that you can only use the biggest part of that experience if you have another job that's the same. In most jobs, you learn a substantial amount at the beginning but then stop and just continue to repeat the same tasks over and over. This creates a stagnant and frustrating cycle of repetition. This is one of the major causes of job dissatisfaction. Creating income that is unique and inventive stimulates the mind and keeps you interested in life.

Something notable and obvious in the corporate environment is the lack of passion. It's as if employees have been beaten into submission. Whose idea was it that gray cubicle walls were the best environment for stimulating, efficient work? Let's call them what they are: They're depressing. It's also demeaning to have your performance evaluated by your boss just to get a pittance of a raise every year. Who can say how much your time is worth, and more importantly, why should you have to prove it and then beg for a few scraps more?

Purely from a dollars and cents standpoint, you have to know that employee income is taxed on a higher percentage basis than any other. Business owners, investors and the self employed all are able to take advantage of tax breaks employees can't access. Employers also consider additional taxes and benefits for employees to be part of your salary, even though it doesn't go into your pocket. While your actual value may be quite high, once all of these costs and benefits are deducted, you get paid a very small portion. By becoming a business owner, even on a part time basis, it enables you to take advantage of these benefits.

Fear can be a powerful force, especially when you consider leaving the perceived safety of your traditional job. The fact is that safety is just perceived. If someone has the power to hand you a pink slip at any moment, then you are not safe at all. However, if you had several sources of income that no one could ever fire you from, you are in full control of your destiny and no one can take that away or change the rules without your approval. You can't have security if you don't have control; and employees have the least control of anyone.

A Poisonous Environment

How many times have you endured an irrational or uninformed boss? Or been frustrated by office politics? Or wondered why the least capable and most annoying employees always seem to get promoted? Being an employee can be extremely stressful. You dread Monday and can't wait until Friday. You're at the mercy of forces you can neither influence nor control and the lack of a creative outlet can be crushing.

This can have the same effect as poison on the mind and body. Your life and spirit can be so destroyed that you feel utterly worthless. This is why employees frequently refer to their work lives as "doing time." It's ironic so many would refer to their jobs with an expression normally used by prisoners. But these employees *feel* like prisoners—and the environment affects them in much the same way. Many corporate employees become institutionalized—just like prisoners, they refuse to believe there is a life outside the limited world they know.

The effect is made more acute by the fact that, for many people, jobs are the primary social outlet in their lives. Thinking of that social network can feel like leaving family. They have so much in common from the experience—both good and, usually, bad—that it can be difficult to have a conversation with anyone not employed by the same company. To break these ties and go out on your own is not just scary; it feels like you're abandoning an entire group of people. In a way you are. You're abandoning their paradigms and ingrained beliefs. And those not prepared for this change can quickly find themselves working a corporate job again.

But it's unnatural to conform yourself to a corporate environment full of meaningless policies. The long list of rules that govern most people's work life is so lengthy you would practically need an advanced degree to decipher it. Those who have learned to fit into this world can hardly believe there's a place where that sort of regulatory governance doesn't exist. They can't imagine that they could make a living without someone standing over them to regulate how they dress, how they talk, who they talk to or what photos they have on their desk.

It's easy for those who have escaped this kind of culture to be dumbfounded that so many view it as the safe and correct path. But with paradigms, social networks and fear to maintain the status quo, it can be extremely hard to break free.

If you are currently a satisfied employee, you might react negatively to this summation. But that resistance is a component of your paradigm. It is the Y idea smacking up against your X beliefs. However, you also know on some level that what I'm telling you is the truth—or you wouldn't have any sort of response at all, let alone an emotional one. Maybe it all happened so gradually that you never noticed it; and now, it's a general numbness of the mind.

If this makes you angry, that's a good thing. Anger is a much stronger emotion than apathy. It's certainly preferable to being numb. Any emotion—even fear—is better than apathy. If you work through these feelings and strive toward the truth, you'll soon experience the courage to change.

Realize you earn income by providing value, not doing time. Find a way to provide value to others and charge a fair price for it. One of the biggest obstacles you'll face is that you may not have any real value to offer others. You may assume that being an employee is the best you can do. Maybe you're concerned you aren't worth that much. This type of thinking is all part of your 'get a job' paradigm—and it's complete nonsense. As you focus on your purpose and visualize your dreams, you'll soon recognize that you have the ability to provide enormous value to others— and that people will gladly pay you for it. There's only one thing that prevents you from immediately seeing this truth: Fear.

You are not your job. It does not define who you are or all that you have to offer. Your real value is based upon who you are, not what you do. The only thing you need to do is express your real self to the world. You've been conditioned to think this is unproductive or that you can't make money at it. But you'll never know true happiness and fulfillment until you find the courage to do it anyway. Learn to trust your inner wisdom, even if the whole world says you're wrong. What do they know anyway? No-one knows you the way you do. Years from now, as you stand on the peak of your mountain, you'll look back and realize it was one of the best decisions you ever made.

Be Your Own Boss

There are plenty of misconceptions about what it's like to be self employed. Interestingly enough, most of these ideas come from people who have *never been* self employed! Again, the paradigms held by the masses have very little to do with reality. I often talk about the reality of self employment, because it means something different to almost everyone. This allows me to dispel a few of the myths and share the knowledge of those who actually know what it's like.

Reality #1
You don't have to work long hours.

It's true that many self employed people work longer hours than employees. In large part, it's because they enjoy what they're doing. When you know your purpose and are focused on reaching your goals, it's vastly different than sitting in a cubicle playing solitaire and waiting on five o'clock. You're energized, productive and excited by the events of the day. You rarely mind putting in some extra time. You know the reward for that time will come to you and you alone—not to your boss or to some nameless, face-less shareholder. The great part about the hours you work is that it's your choice. That flexibility alone is worth much more than a nine-to-five job can offer. If you don't like working long hours, you certainly don't have to.

Reality #2
Self employment does not mean added stress.

The greatest stress most people face is when they can't afford their basic needs. However, given the flexibility and freedom that self employment brings, it's actually much less stressful than a full time job for several reasons:

- You chose when you work and where.
- You choose the people you work with.
- You decide when you take time off.
- You have the ultimate say over everything you do and don't

have to follow policies or procedures that someone else dreamed up.

- There are no performance reviews, probationary periods or vacation requests.
- You decide when you get a raise and how much you are worth.
- You have control over your life and determine what path you will take.

Reality #3
You don't have to sell your business to make money.

During the 1990s, many people started IT and software companies from nothing. They built them up for a few years and cashed out and made millions. This contributed to the idea that, in order to really make your fortune, you have to sell a company. While you can certainly build a business to sell or to take public, you can also build a business to keep that produces steady cash flow for a long period of time. The idea of passive income relies on this type of thinking. You can own multiple businesses at one time and collect money from them all.

You decide what kind of business you want. If you decide you want to be the next Bill Gates, that's great—there are no hard and fast rules. The important thing to understand is that it has to get you to the top of the mountain, no matter what kind of business it is or what kind of cash flow it produces. You are free to choose and that choice opens the door to a multitude of opportunity.

Reality #4
Diversification is Your Friend.

Self employment brings up much talk of risk vs. reward. The bottom line is that human beings feel most secure when they have control. Self-employment gives you control over your income

—far more than you have with a regular job. When you're self-employed, no one can fire you or lay you off. If you need to come up with additional cash very quickly, it can be difficult to do as an employee. But if you are an owner who controls all the assets of your business, then you have the option to redirect resources to increase income should you need to. Self employment also allows you to diversify into other areas or sectors, so that if one income stream slows or disappears, there are others that remain unaffected. Employees are at the mercy of one master—and that master can eliminate your position on a whim.

Reality #5
You choose your customers.

As an employee, you must deal with your employer's customers—whether you like them or not. Many corporations still live by the adage, "The customer is always right." You and I both know that it's not true. There are those customers who want everything free or who are convinced that the more they complain, the more attention and better service they'll get. If you're self-employed, you have the option to get rid of customers that waste your time. Some customers just aren't worth having.

You have the ability to say no to anyone at any time. *You are the boss.* There's no reason to put up with a customer who is threatening or insulting. In some businesses, bad behavior on the part of customers seems to be rewarded. But you don't have to allow it! You make the rules. There's no need to do business with people who think it's their prerogative to treat you poorly. You won't enjoy having them—and you won't enjoy their referrals either.

Reality #6
You have a great social network.

We've touched on the idea that many people fear leaving the social network they've built as an employee. However, if all you do is spend time with other employees, then it won't move you forward, will it? Most—if not all—the people I spend time around are self employed and interested in wealth generation. When you choose to become self-employed, you'll develop new networks with people who can help you and who think as you do. A self-employed person has the time to network during business hours without worrying that they will be reprimanded for socializing too much.

There's no need to feel isolated or alone if you're self-employed. But it's important to build new and strong relationships. You may find these relationships to be stronger than your previous ones; after all, they're with energetic, positive and motivated entrepreneurs. You don't get together to gripe about the boss or that memo from HR. You gather to talk about new ideas that can move you forward and make you even more money.

Self-employment can also allow you to socialize more freely with family and friends all over the world. Since you will no longer have to fit your visits into a long weekend or holiday.

Reality #7
Self-employment is not hard or complicated.

Self-employed people don't have to know how to do everything for a business to succeed—they're just responsible for making sure everything gets done. Newly self-employed people sometimes have a hard time letting go. They find it hard to delegate. However, it's essential if you want to use your time most effectively. Why spend time mowing the lawn when you could be working on a new source of income?

Some people try to make business ownership as difficult as they possibly can. Often, deep in their mind, they might still have the belief that earning money has to be hard. The truth is, it can be as simple as you chose to make it—but it's definitely not hard.

Self-employment can also have the illusion of being very complicated. Taxes, legal organization, insurance and many other details of business ownership can seem overwhelming. There's certainly a learning curve, but these aren't complicated issues—especially for small businesses. As your business grows, you can pay for expert advice if you're uncomfortable. Don't let the initial learning curve intimidate or confuse you. Once you set up and learn the basics with your first business, all of that knowledge will be immediately applicable for you next business—and you will have one!—saving you time and money.

Reality #8
You can start with very little cash.

How much is very little? There are plenty of businesses that you can get into for a very small amount of money. As that business goes up in value, you expand your opportunities. This means you don't have to put everything you have into a business up front to start earning cash. If you create value and provide something that others are interested in, you *will* profit. If you're able to have a specific time investment and get paid repeatedly, then it can also create a steady source of passive income. A good example of this is to write a book. You expend the effort once and it continues to sell for years.

Think about how this sort of concept affects employees. Let's pretend you're a software developer. If you design a system while working for your salary, you get paid the same—whether that program is good or bad it doesn't matter. If it works well, then your employer will make money from it for years. Meanwhile, you move on to develop their next money-making program, but you still get the same salary.

Contrast this with this idea: Develop your own programs and sell them to others. Now you create a new revenue source with each idea you create that benefits you for your entire life. When you look at the two scenarios, you are essentially doing the same work, but in one you get paid a set amount and in the other your income is limitless. All it takes is a good idea and a willingness to work. It doesn't take large amounts of cash, and the rewards are tremendous.

Don't Fear the Unknown

No matter what I tell you or how convincing an argument I make, you still have to choose to set aside the doubts in your mind. I hope that some of these realities will help combat your fears and existing beliefs about what it's really like to be a business owner. Lots of people have nightmares about starving to death on the path of self-employment, but such irrational fears aren't representative of reality. Self-employment is a powerful catalyst for personal growth. Often, the greatest value comes from the lessons and self-confidence you gain along the way. You'll never truly feel the exhilaration of being your own master until you finally let go of the perceived safety of a traditional job. Much like a baby who learns to stand by holding onto furniture, you must eventually be willing to let go in order to walk—and then run.

Fear of the unknown decreases over time. You become used to trusting your own instincts and judgment. But it will never disappear completely. Once you develop a wealthy mindset, though, you'll be able to handle that fear and put it in its place. That's when you'll accomplish your goals.

Chapter 7 REVIEW

- Real change requires strong and continued commitment.
- Accountability increases your chance of success.
- Being successful is not an all or nothing mindset.
- Business ownership allows you to take advantage of significant tax breaks.
- You don't have security if you don't have control.
- Your real value is based upon who you are not what you do.
- Self-employment is a powerful catalyst for personal growth.
- To help others execute these ideas, investigate www.BobProctorMoney.com/LSC

Chapter 8

Speed Up and Calm Down

How often have you felt harassed and traumatized by the pace of life? So much has been written about stress and burnout, and thousands suffer from it every year. We assume people are tired and worn because they are going too fast—that's the easy thing to do. But I've discovered that slowing down and directing my energies with focus allows me to move calmly and with confidence—and get much more accomplished! When you remove worry and uncertainty from your life, you can calmly and swiftly evaluate the steps that will move you toward your goals.

Millions of people long for peace in their lives because they live in absolute chaos. Their relationships are volatile, their careers oppressive, and their finances on the verge of collapse. I promised you at the very beginning of this book that I would tell you the truth; if you are living in chaos right now, I can tell you that it's because you have *chosen to do so*. This may be hard to accept, but if you have any doubts, a quick evaluation will reveal the truth of this.

Take a look at the people you spend time around—family, friends or coworkers. How many of them make large demands on your time? How many of them return the favor, and how many take advantage? Learn the difference, and distance yourself from those who deplete your time to protect your own well-being.

Sometimes this distance only needs to be temporary to be effective; but you can't change your way of thinking if old paradigms surround you. Going on a week-long vacation can be very effective in changing a state of mind. Once you return to your normal life, it will be crystal clear which people in your life are generating the negative energy you need to avoid.

If you dread your job each and every day, why do you stay? Have you ever tried to earn some sort of passive income and rescue yourself—or do you just accept it as your lot in life? If you are reading this book, you have probably read others about wealth creating; but have you really tried anything that these books have suggested? You left them on the shelf to gather dust.

Finances are the main source of chaos in most people's lives. But they keep doing things that create *even more chaos*. Because they have a mindset of lack, they focus all their energies on what they don't have. And what do they attract into their lives? More of the same. They end up engaging in behaviors that escalate their debt, and devalue their time.

Take Amy as an example:

I was in my late twenties and a single mother when I felt my life had spun out of control. I dated men who were emotionally needy and demanded a lot of time. My daughter was four and a constant source of stress. I couldn't seem to get her to do anything I asked.

I'd worked as a billing clerk for four years and made very little money. I was always strapped for cash. I never seemed to be able to have the things other people didn't think twice about. I'd never even been able to take a vacation. I spent my days off at home worrying how to make ends meet the next month.

One summer my boss asked if I'd be interested in helping a friend of hers on weekends as a personal assistant. I jumped at the idea, thinking that this could give me a little bit of extra money. The woman's name was Linda, and she worked out of her home, running a network marketing business.

I went to her home every weekend. I was just astounded at how this woman lived. She didn't seem to worry about anything! I couldn't comprehend it. Money seemed to flow directly to her like magic. I watched her closely, trying to figure out what made her so special; but she seemed, well, normal. I just didn't get it. After a few weeks, my frustration finally got the best of me. I blurted out that it just wasn't fair—life was so easy for her, and so hard for me.

Linda sat me down. She was very direct. She said that I was a virtual Chaos Magnet, and that my results were due to the way I thought about life. She said over and over that I'd created the life I was living, and that the only way I would ever change was to choose to change my thoughts.

I went home and cried my eyes out—not because she was wrong, but because she was right. I had done this to myself. I could look back and pinpoint every single choice I made that put me right where I was.

That summer was a turning point. I learned to remove the chaos from my life and create a wealthy mindset. I joined the same company as Linda, and grew my own business with her guidance. The new, calm confidence that I gained attracted different people into my life. Soon, I had a supportive and loving partner. As I reduced or eliminated my unimportant activities, and chose to inject more calm into my life, my daughter suddenly became more obedient. She had been suffering from the negative chaos I had created, and her rebellion was how she demonstrated the stress.

My life is now peaceful and serene. I no longer worry about money. I will never be a Chaos Magnet again!

Before she took responsibility for her situation, Amy complained that life was unfair. This is pretty common. But she found that it was completely fair: *She had made the choices that created what she was currently experiencing as chaos.* You can choose chaos, or you can choose peace—it all hinges on the willingness to take responsibility. And that's up to you!

Ignoring the Unimportant

Remember when we talked about prioritizing your activities? We said that you should reduce or eliminate as many unimportant tasks as you can. This will give you time and energy to focus on your path—the path that will lead you to your goals. I can confidently say that as much as 50% of what most people do every day is completely unimportant in the grand scheme of things. I'll also tell you how hard it is to avoid getting sucked in by urgent little tasks. You seem to face them constantly, I know. They just won't go away, and it can take some practice to learn to say no. At the very least, put them off to a better time so you don't get distracted from what's important.

A great deal has been written on the subject of multitasking—the ability to do many things at once. Some suggest that this is a way to be more efficient. This is one of the great fallacies of our era. If you split your focus, you can't do any of the tasks very well. And this split focus can be very dangerous indeed. Think of driving and talking on your cellphone, all while reading a map! You won't really know where you're going, you won't have much of a conversation—and you might find yourself off the road!

Think of this as a metaphor for the new path you're trying to create. There's chatter in your ear and you don't really know where you're going—but you're going nonetheless. Think about which of these is most important: Naturally, I would say the map. But how many people have you driven by, chatting away, one hand on the wheel, map spread on their laps? They've chosen to believe that, by cramming more actions on top of actions, they are getting more or better results.

Like most other paradigms accepted by the masses, this is completely backward. Why do you think that most very wealthy people hire someone to drive them where they need to go? So they can concentrate on something else and use that time effectively without risking their lives. They understand the power of focusing completely in order to have the best outcome.

Even if we're using our time very effectively through focusing on our goals, it doesn't mean that we should just go, go, go. Your mind needs rest; so you need to find a balance, alternating between action, evaluation and rest. Often, when we go as fast as we can, it's just a mask for fear; we think that, if we cram as much as we can into every minute, then we'll surely succeed. But if you slow down and really look at what you're accomplishing, you'll see that you are doing everything—except what's really important. You can't achieve great results through sheer volume of activity; so much of this activity is wasted energy.

There is a quote by Mohandas Gandhi I like very much: "There is more to life than increasing its speed." Advances in technology have sped our lives up substantially in the past century, and certainly, it has improved our lives. But it also increases the chance that low priority, and mundane activities will compete with truly important ones for our time. The result is a frantic and chaotic lifestyle. There are just so many tasks we can accomplish; too many of us take this as justification that we need to do all of them.

We may think these are tiny things that don't take much time or effort; but we waste so much energy separating and prioritizing all these tasks. Expending this energy steals from energy that should be devoted to important tasks—the ones that move us to our goals.

This 'do everything' mindset creates a panic: the more you try to do, the greater that panic increases; you feel the horrible stress of being "behind." This is why it is so important to step back and prioritize. You have to be willing to let the unimportant go; after all, you'll need your sanity if you want to accomplish anything significant!

You need to understand that, while you have the power to choose, you simply can't choose everything. Think of small children in a candy shop. They want to have everything, but their hands—and stomachs!—only hold so much. Even realizing this, you'll see them grabbing new things, dropping others—still trying to do the impossible, and making a mess because of it. And this can go on for hours! If the child's parent had told them at the beginning they could only have one or two, he or she would have spent time evaluating which one they really wanted. It would have made them focus—and the goal, of getting the best candy that brings about the most satisfaction, would have been accomplished that much quicker, taking much less time and energy.

Now think of that situation in terms of your own life. Set rules for yourself the same way. You know there is a limited amount of time; you have to have a way to evaluate what you do with it, or you accomplish nothing. You need to have wisdom to effectively evaluate the tasks, and integrity and fortitude to make the critical tradeoffs for those things you must let go.

The Importance of Critical Thinking

The masses are fascinated by the sensational. The tedious details of celebrity lives provide a steady stream of mindless drivel that more and more people accept as their normal media diet. The more controversial and outlandish, the more attention it receives. Even though the very people who live their lives with this sort of notoriety often destroy themselves, millions dream of being just like them. They mimic the behavior they see, and often bring tremendous amounts of drama and stress to their lives.

Those who seek wealth cannot be pulled into this drama. They must learn to think critically. This includes identifying and evaluating our existing paradigms. Which ones help you, which hold you back? Where did they come from and what is the real truth that needs to be acknowledged for real change to happen?

We all think, all the time. However, much of our thinking is a direct reflection of the ideas we've accumulated, and the paradigms we've created and accepted as a result. We rarely stop and question these assumptions before we allow them to affect our lives and influence our results. For this reason, much of your thinking will be biased, distorted, partial, uninformed or downright wrong.

Now think about it: The quality of your life depends precisely on the quality of your thoughts. Poor thinking is costly, both in terms of money and in quality of life. Excellence in thought, however, can be learned and actively cultivated.

Critical thinking is not innate or natural in anyone. Even those who are normally very critical in their thought process can be subject to episodes of undisciplined or irrational thought. This is especially true with very emotional moments, or thoughts that challenge a deeply held paradigm.

Quality thought is typically a matter of degree. Among other things, it depends on the quality and depth of experience in a given area. No one is a critical thinker through-and-through; critical thinking is achievable only to a particular level, and that level can change. For this reason, the development of critical thinking skills is a life-long endeavor. You never stop learning or improving your skills to think critically—nor should you be too hard on yourself for the occasional lapse.

I can't stress this enough: Critical thinking involves continual learning. I consider myself a lifetime student of all areas of personal growth. No one can ever learn all there is to know about how we think, or what motivates us to live our dreams. But we can all be students of life. This means exploring new ideas; whether that's done by reading, listening, watching, conversing, learning from others, or actually trying—perhaps starting a new business. We should all keep our minds open to what each and every one of these activities can teach us.

Lifelong learning is a willingness to keep exploring the many adventures that life has to offer. The benefits of this willingness are tremendous. You develop a greater enthusiasm for life. Your self esteem increases, along with your self-respect. You're more interested and engaged in the world around you. Perhaps most importantly, you are a conduit for new ideas that you can pass on to those around you. You become what you seek—an instrument for life-long learning.

What About Self-acceptance?

I'm often asked how to balance self-acceptance with the urge for growth and development of a wealthy mindset. It's important to aim for improvement in every area of life. But we all start at different levels on the ascent to a wealthy mindset. Remember that there is no reason to feel badly if someone seems to be ascending more quickly than you—and more importantly, those kinds of feelings of self-doubt are very counter-productive, as the *law of attraction* shows us.

It's also no excuse to give up and accept where you are. The point of the journey you've begun is to understand why you are the way you are, and what concepts shape your thoughts. Critically appraising your situation, and how you got there, is very different from using self-acceptance as an excuse to hide and never try.

Most people are caught somewhere in between being fully committed to their goals and accepting their current lot. Lots of people hold on to the idea that, if you commit to improving yourself every day, you obviously don't accept who you are today. Nonsense!

These ideas stem from the same backward thinking—and they

are just as wrong! If you accept responsibility for your decisions and the results you have achieved in your life so far, you'll be far more able to move on and make better decisions that produce better results.

A huge stumbler with self-acceptance for most people is simply that they don't see themselves accurately to begin with. They'll have a warped—and often negative—self-image, which prevents them from seeing things in realistic terms. Our self-image is developed over our whole lives, and it changes over time. If you've ever had the same problems with money surface time and again, or you had a business that failed or had to declare bankruptcy, you may develop the idea that you're no good with money and it's hopeless to try.

By now, I hope you know this simply isn't true. The tools for managing money can be learned by anyone. So you're not "bad with money"—you just never learned how to manage it, or attract it into your life. It can easily be fixed—but if you've developed a self-image with this idea of being "bad with money" as an absolute, you may never accept what's really possible.

Self-image is the personal view you have of yourself. If it's negative, it hampers your attempt to change. Your self-image allows you to create labels that describe who you are, and what you can do. These labels might include things like smart, wealthy, and creative. They might also include things like stupid, fat, or worthless. These labels form an overall view of the balance of our good and bad qualities.

Self-image is a learned assumption of who we are. Parents and teachers often make the first and greatest contribution to our overall self-image. How they respond to us and treat us develops the picture in our mind of who we are. As we're exposed to friends and relatives, this image becomes more defined. By the time we reach adulthood, relationships and experiences reinforce what we think and feel about ourselves.

The image you see in your mind could be an accurate reflection of who you are, but most often, it's distorted. The strengths and weaknesses learned as a child become internalized, and affect your results as an adult. This self-image is not static; it is dynamic and ever-changing. We constantly evaluate how others respond to us, and how we feel about that response. We compare ourselves, and develop an idea of where we rank. This gives us a sense of our overall value to others, and to society as a whole.

The fact that your self-image can be changed allows you to develop a healthier and more accurate view of yourself; this means you can also alter the distortions that limit your progress. But to effect this change, you must first be able to step back and evaluate your own self-image.

What ideas do you have about yourself and what labels have you created? Let's take this one: "I'm stupid." This often stems from something you heard, or a specific incident when you were young that caused embarrassment or fear. Children frequently interpret these emotions as "feeling stupid." As this mental label is carried forward, it seems natural to assume that you are stupid; and you limit yourself believing that difficult things aren't worth even trying, because you can't possibly succeed.

This is an awful circumstance, made even more so by how far from the truth it really is. First, you have to understand that you are just as smart as anyone else. And besides, as we've discussed, you don't have to be a genius, or have a great deal of education, to become wealthy. You need to also look at all of the labels that you have for yourself, and realize they may well stem from a childhood assumption that is completely unfounded.

Next, you have to stop ranking yourself. This is an internal version of the comparison paradox: You judge whether you are smart, beautiful or well-off compared to those around you. This is how most of us come up with the idea that we are average: in comparison to our peers, we seem about the same.

But you're a unique and individual person. Your worth cannot be measured by comparison to *anyone*: *There is no-one else who is exactly like you*. In other words, you're priceless and incomparable. How could you ever consider that you would be worth less than anyone else?

For a number of years, I have told audiences all over the world that, if they want to live a healthier, happier, more productive life, they should learn how to maintain calmness. To achieve this, there are two things I recommend. There is a lady I know who teaches this better than anyone else I know. She is not connected with our company and I receive no material compensation for recommending her. I mention that because she is very good and I encourage you to take advantage of her services. Visit www.calmconfidence.com.

And, secondly, in his classic, *As A Man Thinketh*, James Allen has dedicated the last chapter to Serenity. I encourage you to rewrite this chapter by hand, carry it with you and read it twice a day—just after you wake up and just before you go to sleep. Visit www.bobproctor.com for a free download of Serenity.

Accepting Challenge

Different people define hard work in different ways. Some think of hard work only in terms of physical exertion; others would consider finding solutions to difficult problems to be hard work. I think of it as anything that requires focused effort and stretches your idea of what is possible—or in other words, that which challenges you.

This challenge can be either physical or mental; often, it's both. Challenges move you from the comfort of what you know, and they force you to creatively find solutions for the unknown. Challenge is important: It keeps you from becoming complacent and doing what is easiest—rather than what is best. The masses go down the wide road of 'easy,' while the few struggle along the path to true wealth. This is partly why, when challenges come, you'll often feel very alone. Everyone else gives up and runs back to that wide, easy road.

Big challenges are frequently accompanied by big results. The more focused effort it takes to climb your mountain, the greater the feeling of elation when you plant your flag on the summit. When you commit to do what others won't, you will produce results that they will never know. I once saw an interview with a survivor of a plane crash. He said, "There is no greater elation than the joy you feel after avoiding certain death." Great challenges can produce similar feelings of accomplishment. The desire and willingness to do what seems too hard for others will give you access to the great treasures of life.

Great challenges require great perseverance. Ask yourself, 'how many times can I be knocked down and still get up and keep going?' What's your limit? When will you call it quits? Have you given yourself a timeline for success? If it doesn't work, will you go back to what you were doing before? Have you imagined a worst-case scenario that will give you an excuse to not try again?

If you have, then you are giving yourself a reason to fail. You are hedging your bets rather than giving it 100%. And you know what? You're right—you *will* fail. You can't start out with the idea that you'll try it for a year and let yourself give up. You have to give it everything you have and determine in your own mind there is no going back. If you don't give yourself the opportunity to quit, then you simply have to move forward.

Perseverance is tied very closely to belief. If you can hold the image of your goal in your mind and focus your energy, you are persisting in that belief and it will happen. This belief creates the self-discipline needed to keep you on task; it will not allow you to falter or become apathetic. Imagine if you decided to lose 30 pounds. Every week, you get on the scale and you see continual progress. That progress fuels the discipline by enhancing the belief that you will reach your goal. It's the same in the area of wealth: Each small accomplishment provides the energy to rise to the next level. As you climb higher and higher, you can look back and see solid evidence of how far you've come. This gives you a huge emotional boost for your efforts.

Chapter 8 REVIEW

- Remove the chaos from your life.
- Learn to say no to the unimportant.
- Reduce multitasking and focus your energies.
- Alternate between action, evaluation and rest.
- Learn to think critically.
- Self-image is a learned assumption of who you are.
- Big challenges are accompanied by big results.

Chapter 9

Leverage Your Love and Really Live

The time to start on the path to wealth is right now—this very minute. You don't have to know everything, and you don't need a perfect plan. Everyone wants to know how to escape from his or her own *Prison of Perception*; we all want to set out on the path to freedom. You may feel like you are imprisoned behind solid steel bars, but the truth is that the door to your personal jail cell isn't locked—it never was. Nothing binds you to the results you've had, and are currently having, but the chains in your own mind. You're completely free to choose a new and exciting path.

Once you start creating your own stream of income and allowing money to flow through your life, you will find that you can increase this flow by getting help from others. As you focus on your strengths and prioritize your tasks, you'll want to delegate those tasks that others can perform better than you can. Imagine you have one acorn to plant. This seed is planted and all its energy is put into producing a tree. No matter how big or beautiful that tree may be, it can only become one tree. However, if your tree produces acorns and each of those becomes another tree, you soon have an entire forest. All those other acorns are people that can help you become wealthy. They may be assistants, accountants, lawyers, web designers, or any of hundreds of other people. They allow you to leverage your time exponentially.

Your Wealth Team

Everyone around you has a specific body of knowledge. All of this can help you achieve your goals. Creating trust through relationships allows you to gain access to their knowledge and produces a mutually-beneficial arrangement. Most small businesspeople start out doing most of the work themselves. As they grow, they often use contractors to help with the more mundane tasks, allowing them to purchase the exact services they need without taking on the responsibility of employees. This is the beginning of the creation of your wealth team.

Wealthy individuals have long known about the powerful concept of leveraging other people's time. They have all applied and used this principle to gain their own wealth. This is not to say you take advantage of anyone; rather, you become involved in a relationship that benefits both sides. As you build your wealth team, you'll find those who offer you their time in exchange for money, or your skills. Leverage creates a win-win situation for everyone involved.

By owning your own business, you can use this leverage. It's an adjustment from being a one person show, but you'll never grow or expand your ability to earn money unless you get help. It's too time-consuming to build a business without leveraging the resources of other people. You need their time and abilities. Understanding leverage and how it can work for you is a key step to understanding money and amassing wealth.

Building your wealth team means assessing each person's natural abilities and strengths, and assigning projects or jobs that best suit those natural abilities. Some people are creative problems-solvers; some are detail oriented; others can manage several projects at once. Not everyone has these skills, so it makes sense to put these people in positions that will allow them to excel. They enjoy their work and have a great sense of accomplishment while moving the whole business forward, which makes them all the more productive. This is exactly the kind of leverage that you must understand and employ to reach your financial goals.

Communication

As you begin to work with others, you'll find one of the biggest challenges to be effective communication. You have to convey your wishes effectively; but you also have to be open to what others have to say. Not everyone realizes that the most important aspect of creating relationships with others—be they employees, customers, contractors or anyone else—begins with listening.

Many people confuse hearing with listening, and they end up failing to understand the message being presented. This can damage the relationship, as it tends to leave people feeling insignificant and frustrated. Needless to say, this is not good for your progress. If you continue to discount their thoughts, they will become emotionally distant and you will cease to have their full cooperation and creative ideas.

Listening takes attention, focus and the willingness to accept what you're being told. It also requires you to be aware of what is NOT being said; a great deal of communication is conveyed non-verbally, through body language. Listening effectively is *not* a passive activity. Our brains work much faster than our ability to speak, so we often jump way ahead of the conversation in our minds and miss the opportunity to fully understand that person's feelings, opinions and perspective. Distractions and assumptions can interfere with what is being said, so work hard to concentrate on that person and really absorb their words and gestures.

Listening is really a gift of your time, as is the attention you give to another person. It is your obligation to respond both verbally and non-verbally to that person. It lets them know that you're actively listening and absorbing what they're saying; and that you understand what they are trying to communicate. This is how you let them know you value what's being said, and by doing so, it opens their heart and creative mind to fully communicate.

The skill of listening can, and should be, cultivated. I've listed a few common errors and important points to learn if you want to improve your listening abilities:

1. **Silence is Golden.** This may seem obvious, but many people are impatient. They focus not on what is being said, but are calculating their response and waiting for their chance to speak. They only listen for a few minutes before interrupting, which cuts off the flow of communication. Be courteous and give the other person your full attention. Avoid the natural tendency to immediately offer solutions or opinions. Just listen.

2. **Receive the Entire Message.** A good listener looks interested in what others are saying. You must also be aware that your body language is very important. Maintain eye contact, sit still, lean slightly toward the other person, and nod your head on occasion to convey that you understand the points they're making.

3. **Repeat Points or Ask Questions.** Listen closely and when the other person pauses, this is a good time to verify what you think you heard, or ask questions to clarify anything you didn't understand. You can do this by paraphrasing what you heard. Ask if it's correct. This gives the person the opportunity to clear up anything you misunderstood. It also allows them to hear what their message sounds like from your perspective.

4. **Be aware of physical barriers.** It's very important to be at eye level with the person speaking, if possible. Don't allow them to stand while you sit, or the other way around. If you

sit at a desk, be sure to move to some comfortable chairs so it doesn't present a perceived barrier between you. This will make the conversation more open and honest.

5. **Respect the Person.** No matter the message, some conversations should not be public - especially if they involve criticism or personal issues. Be sure to respect each person's private information and closely guard what he or she tells you in confidence. This will help them trust you and feel more at ease because they know that you respect them as a person.

6. **Respect Their Feelings.** Even if you don't agree with what the person it trying to tell you, avoid defensive statements or words. You must accept what is being said without argument. Later, you can take time to review what was said and formulate a response. As a good listener, you should allow the person the time and space to fully express his or her feelings. No matter how much you may disagree, that doesn't mean that their feelings aren't real or valid. To brush off or invalidate those feelings crushes their spirit and creates animosity; this will do nothing to help you achieve your goals.

7. **Show Gratitude.** Thank the person for sharing their thoughts and feelings. Be genuine. It takes great courage to speak up and be heard—especially if they're pointing out something that needs improving. Honest communication builds trust and encourages further dialogue.

8. **Opportunity for Growth.** Feedback and opinions from others present an opportunity for growth. It must be met with an open mind. For this reason, it is important to evaluate all points made, not just those you agree with. You should never be too busy to listen to someone else's opinion or point of view.

It takes time and effort to become a good listener. But as you improve these skills, your patience will be rewarded. As you become a more effective listener, you might be surprised to find people will seek you out to share their thoughts and feelings. You'll also notice you're involved in fewer conflicts, and become perceived as an honest and trustworthy person. Attentive listening is a unique skill that people respect and admire.

The other side of listening is the ability to convey your own thoughts and desires effectively. Like listening, speaking in a way that is easily understood is not as simple as it sounds. Verbal communication requires you to put your thoughts into clear chunks of information that can be easily absorbed. Long-winded stories and speeches about nothing can cause the listener to become tired, lose interest and shift focus, resulting in a communication breakdown.

There may also be times when you hold yourself back from expressing yourself because of self-doubt or fear. This is very common, especially if you are starting a new business, or are working in an unfamiliar area. I know plenty of people who seem to become mute when they meet with their accountant. They are so unfamiliar with tax laws that they're afraid to ask questions for fear of showing their ignorance. Effective communication means finding the courage to speak up—even if you might sound foolish or repeat information that the listener may already know. You've heard the adage "there are no stupid questions"? It's true! By remaining silent, you deny yourself the opportunity to learn and grow.

Relationships are a careful balance between speaking effectively and listening fully. When communication is based on honesty, respect, and good intentions, each person feels accepted and valued. Good communication skills allow you to solve conflicts and share accomplishments. As a result, your professional and personal relationships will be nurtured and enhanced.

Mending Fences

There will always be moments when relationships are strained in some way. This could happen with customers, clients, employees, or vendors. If these problems aren't dealt with swiftly and effectively, they can grow to a seemingly-insurmountable mountain. I say 'seemingly' because it's easy to assume a relationship is completely irreparable, but that is rarely the case. Most often, the original issue is quite minor—the real problem is in how it was handled and that is what creates a great deal of negative emotion. It is this emotion that must be diffused before the relationship can move forward.

Think of a customer with a complaint. They send an email, nicely worded, to request help. You don't respond. They email again, and their communication becomes more heated; they insist on a response. If they still don't get satisfaction, they might start to call. No matter what your intentions, silence or lack of response is interpreted as lack of respect or caring. Suddenly, you receive a letter from their attorney. This is exactly the path that many small issues travel to escalate into ridiculous battles. This is why it is so important to pay attention!

Prevention is the best avenue for mending fences. By making it a priority to respond to small issues, your customers and vendors will remain happy, and your relationships with them healthy. In fact, your ability to respond quickly to issues will generate a reputation of responsibility and more people will want to work with you and seek you out.

It is important to understand that the underlying problem is not the original issue that the customer or vendor raised. The real problem is the emotion that that person attached to your actions or lack of action. As time goes on, the original issue doesn't escalate. It remains what it was at the outset. But the emotion attached to it grows based on how satisfied they are with your response. Emotion can create or destroy relationships, because emotions affect the perception of those involved—including your own. You can be the one upset rather than the customer or vendor and your emotions can escalate with a minimal amount of provocation just as easily.

When you have a relationship that moves to shaky ground, there are several things you can do to bring it back to stability. First, try to assess the situation objectively. That means determining how much of the problem involves real issues, and how much involves emotions. These two areas are handled differently. Usually you will find the original issue is only 10-20% of the conflict, and the rest is emotion.

When dealing with emotions, whether yours or someone else's, it's important to understand that we all have different triggers. Often, these triggers come from experiences or beliefs we've formed in our own minds. This produces differences in expectation levels—often the basis for a misunderstanding in the first place.

No matter what the exact nature of these beliefs, this is no time to assess blame. The important part is that the relationship must be repaired. In order for this to happen, you have to be willing to make the first move. This can be hard; we can be proud and stubborn—especially if we think we're 'right.' If you feel wronged, it can be difficult to engage that person again.

But it can also be very satisfying to make that first move, even when you believe in your heart that you did nothing wrong in the first place. Chances are, the other person believes he or she did nothing wrong either, so if no one makes the first move to repair the relationship, it will just disintegrate. From that point forward, the event becomes a negative porthole, reinforcing the emotions each time you think of it.

There isn't much time or attention paid to the idea of forgiveness within a business environment. This is truly a shame, because it's very important. For many, 'business' mode means you're cold and calculating. This is ridiculous, and far from the truth; what's more, it's impossible—no matter how hard you try! We are human; by this simple fact, we're emotional creatures. Trying to tune out or turn off those emotions makes you an ineffective communicator; in so doing, it damages your ability to create a wealthy mindset.

If you have a bad experience you may hold on to the emotion associated with it, perhaps even replay the scenario in your head. By doing so, you create new negative beliefs for yourself. As we've already discussed, beliefs are powerful and affect you for a very long time. You're also focusing on the event, and attracting similar events through the *Law of Attraction*. The only way to stop this process is to practice forgiveness and let go of the emotion. Forgiveness doesn't justify the behaviour of someone who has wronged you, or betray any of your principles; it simply means you're allowing yourself to move forward emotionally in a positive direction.

Things will go wrong. We will say things we regret, or act without considering how it will affect others without meaning to. And we'll make honest mistakes. You can't approach business or life with an all-or-nothing mindset, or allow yourself to blow events out of proportion. Keep your heart open and forgive indiscretions and errors.

I'm a big believer in second chances. There have been many occasions where I was given a second chance, and I've found it very prudent to do the same for others. Often, those that made a mistake or misstep will have an even closer bond to you if given the chance to make things right.

I like the analogy that most problems are like icebergs. Maybe 5% of them are actual events. The other 95% are your own perception. But that 95% is subject to your conscious control. You can feed your problems with fear and turn them into overwhelming threats, or you can shrink them by stepping back and broadening your perspective. When you artificially inflate your problems, you reduce your ability to solve them. Enlarging your perspective allows you to reduce the problems in your mind. They soon become relatively easy to either solve or accept.

This can be a good time to talk to a mentor or trusted advisor. A third party will rarely have an emotional attachment to the situation and can help you shift your own perspective.

A Grateful Heart

A wealthy mindset is impossible without gratitude, and gratitude is impossible without a wealthy mindset—it doesn't matter what your bank balance is. Gratitude is linked to your mindset and perception of life. Those who have developed and cultivated a wealthy mindset know that there are stages of gratitude, and that it deepens over time.

We are taught as children to be grateful—to be polite and say thank you for gifts and gestures. But for most children, this gratitude is cursory. Not until adulthood do we feel the basic stage of true gratitude. Why? Because it's not until you're on your own that you realize the sacrifices others have made to get you where you are. You realize that they have given you more than you could ever repay, in word or deed; and that's when we experience the emotion of true gratitude for the first time.

This emotion gives you a feeling of wealth. It is deep and heartfelt, but still in the early stages. You're grateful for what you have received from others, but you don't have the deep emotion to be truly grateful for all things yet. I've heard many people say that, in order to create wealth, you must be grateful. This is true. But the gratitude must be deep and emotional to attract that wealth. Lip service provides no energy or vibration for the attraction of wealth.

Often, I've seen people make lists of things they're thankful for: their business, possessions, or the people around them. They read their lists each day, and express their gratitude. This is a good practice, but it can be ineffective if the list is read with no emotion attached to it. This is especially true if that person is actually feeling complacent or negative about their circumstances.

You cannot use lists of things for which you are grateful in an attempt to convince the universe to deliver wealth to your door. You have to become emotionally involved for that to happen. If your gratitude is dependent on your circumstances, it will be temporary at best. Any adverse encounter or event will completely remove it from your thoughts.

Developing a deep and abiding sense of gratitude that is separate from any circumstance or situation is the only way you'll attract wealth. This type of gratitude is for things like life, and creation as a whole. It encompasses everything that you might experience—good or bad. When you have a deep and emotional sense of gratitude, you'll perceive every event as an opportunity for growth, and this will enhance your ability to attract wealth. This type of gratitude is not a temporary activity. It becomes embedded in your sub-conscious; it's a part of who you are, and how you function.

If your gratitude is dependent on those things in life that are material and fleeting—like your possessions, your business or your income—your mindset doesn't change. But when it's centered in the permanent and ever-present, it becomes a permanent and ever-present part of *you*. The easiest way to recognize this change is to notice how you express your gratitude. Instead of listing the things you are grateful for, you write one sentence on your list: "I am grateful." You're not grateful for *anything* in particular; you're simply grateful for *everything*, period.

To manifest this gratitude in your life, you have to practice. Practice by choosing things that are not dependent on circumstance, and say it out loud: "I am grateful for the limitless potential that lies within me." By doing so, you'll move that gratitude to a deeper and more unconditional stage.

When you are living the wealthy life that you dream about, this unconditional gratitude is what you experience. By practicing it now, you are attracting the circumstances that will create that life.

Your Wealth Awaits

> *The way to get started is to start doing.*
> *—Walt Disney*

Within the pages of this book, I've talked about the actions, thoughts and qualities possessed by people who have established their wealthy mindsets. And I'm sure that, by now, you understand why creating wealth is not about the money; it's about how you think and what you create with those thoughts. Now it's time for you to implement these techniques into your own life.

By practicing and building upon the ideas and techniques I've presented, you will be well on your way to a new and glorious life. One day as you stand looking back at the events of your life, you will understand that you had the power to create wealth within you all along. You will know that your accomplishments came from a small seed of belief that now permeates your life.

I encourage you to embrace your own uniqueness and manifest true wealth in your life today. Make the decision—and then get in the dinghy and row!

Chapter 9 REVIEW

- You are completely free to choose a new and exciting path.
- Creating relationships is key to creating wealth.
- Prevention is the best avenue for mending fences.
- Practice forgiveness and let go of emotion.
- Enlarging your perspective allows you to reduce the size of the problems.
- Practice unconditional gratitude.

IT'S NOT ABOUT THE MONEY

BOB PROCTOR
Chairman, LifeSuccess Productions

For over forty years my company has focused on all aspects of personal and professional development for corporations and individuals. If you have a desire to improve your business or the quality of your life personally, please visit www.bobproctoreducation.com and discover what we have to offer.

We welcome the opportunity to serve you.

We operate all around the world.
If you can tell us what you want,
we can show you how to get it!

OUR PURPOSE

"To cultivate and maintain a creative, prosperous environment that inspires and attracts like-minded individuals to learn the Laws of the Mind as they Mastermind together to create and develop Multiple Sources Of Income in a global marketplace."

For further information on the Chairman's Club,
visit www.bobproctoreducation.com